Journal of the Third Daughter

To: Ted & Pat Carney
Blessings

Dec. 25, 2009

Frances L. Peterson
Isaiah 26:3

Journal of the Third Daughter

By Frances L. Peterson

Four Seasons Publishers
Titusville, FL

Journal of The Third Daughter

This work is nonfiction. The characters are real people, names and identifying information have been changed.

For information contact: Four Seasons Publishers
P.O.Box 51, Titusville, FL 32781

PRINTING HISTORY
First Printing 2000

ISBN 1-891929-38-0

PRINTED IN THE UNITED STATES OF AMERICA
1 2 3 4 5 6 7 8 9 10

A Tradition

In Korean culture the third daughter is very special. It is said that when arranging a marriage there is no need to look at her face. She will be very beautiful with a sweet disposition and become a fine wife, dutiful daughter-in-law, and good mother. I was the sixth child of eight and the third daughter. Fact or fancy, I always felt loved and priviledged.

Frances L. Peterson

Foreword

A delight to read, these charming vignettes of life of an American child growing up in a missionary family in rugged northern Korea open windows on a little-known side of overseas missions. They show how in the early decades of this century a whole generation of expatriate Americans discovered other worlds and other cultures.

Stories of their hardships, mistakes, and triumphs abound, but what about their children? They were caught between two worlds and often not quite sure to which they really belonged. Did the experience harm them? Were they hostages to their parents' overriding sense of duty? Statistics indicate quite the contrary. "Mishkids" proved to be consistently above average in later life achievements, and Fran Peterson shows us why.

Frances Lampe Peterson was the "third daughter" among eight children of one of the pioneer Presbyterian missionary couples in an outlying station. Her lively reminiscences reveal kids growing up in a happy family with a sense of humor that lightened the sober austerities of the faith and obedience that had brought their parents to the "ends of the earth." Her chapters ripple with love and laughter. Henry and Ruth Lampe were perseverers and survivors. They prayed and stayed while colleagues were martyred, foreigners harassed by Japanese colonialists, converts persecuted.

They cried and laughed and multiplied and raised a remarkable family whose story is a refreshing reminder that the Christian home—stable, loving, and disciplined—is the linchpin of a healthy society.

Samuel Hugh Moffett

Henry W. Luce Professor of Ecumenics and Missions, Emeritus

Table of Contents

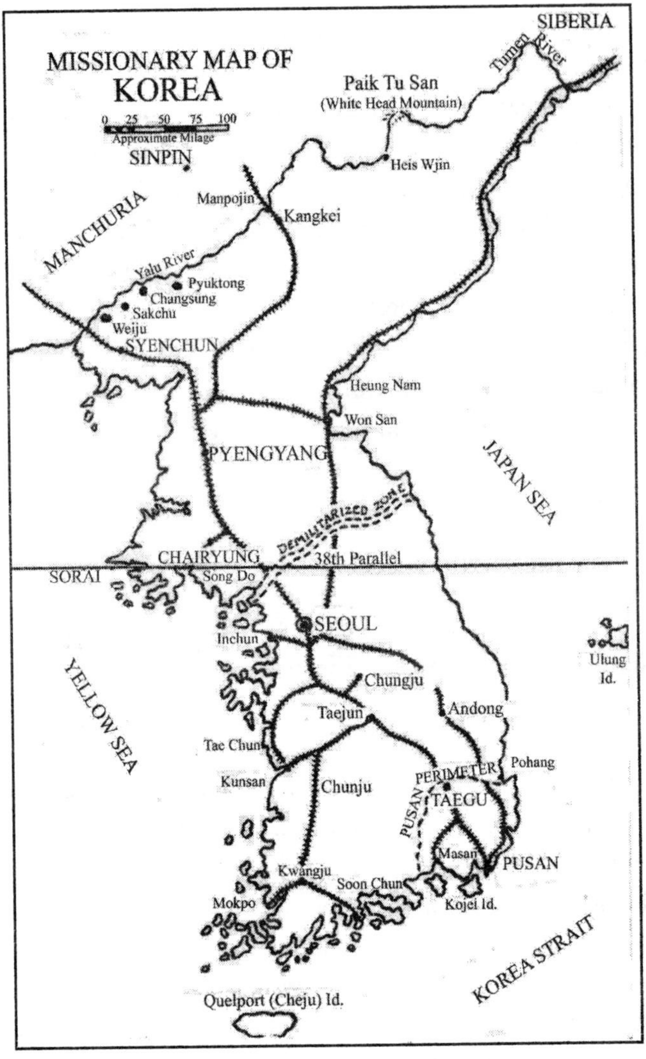
MISSIONARY MAP OF
KOREA
0 25 50 75 100
Approximate Milage
SINPIN
SIBERIA
Tumen River
Paik Tu San
(White Head Mountain)
Heis Wjin
Manpojin
Kangkei
MANCHURIA
Yalu River
Pyuktong
Changsung
Sakchu
Weiju
SYENCHUN
Heung Nam
Won San
JAPAN SEA
PYENGYANG
DEMILITARIZED ZONE
CHAIRYUNG
38th Parallel
SORAI
Song Do
SEOUL
Inchun
Ulung
Id.
YELLOW SEA
Chungju
Andong
Taejun
Tae Chun
Pohang
PERIMETER
Kunsan
Chunju
PUSAN
TAEGU
Masan
PUSAN
Kwangju
Soon Chun
Mokpo
Kojei Id.
KOREA STRAIT
Quelport (Cheju) Id.

Prologue

Whom shall I send, and who will go for us?
Then I said, "Here am I. Send me!"
Is. 6:8

Holding hands they walked down the country lane to settle on their favorite bench under some big sugar maples.

"I understand why your parents are set against my taking you to Korea, Ruth," Henry said. "We haven't any choice but to wait the two years they've requested."

"My heart aches to think of your being away for so long, dearest," she answered, "but you're right. They don't see why you can't stay right here as our pastor. Everybody thinks highly of you, and so do they—but not of the place you want to take me. They're afraid they'll never see me again!" Thus it was that on a beautiful day in May of 1908, Henry Lampe[1] and Ruth Heydon, who were to be my parents, unhappily said good-bye.

Henry was a striking figure, a brand-new, bachelor Presbyterian missionary who stood six feet tall. His light-brown wavy hair and blue eyes were most attractive, but his face was interesting rather than handsome. As a child he took a tumble, landing head first on an upturned rake. It knocked out a front tooth that was never replaced,

[1] Pronounced Lamp, the "e" is silent.

so Mother Nature rearranged his mouth, pushing another tooth into the middle. Somehow I never noticed it until I was a teenager.

He spent his first year in Seoul studying Korean and preached his first sermon on December 17, 1909. It's not an easy language to master, so he must have been both bright and very diligent.

He was assigned to Won Ju, capital of Kangwon Province east of Seoul, where the Presbyterians had bought a station site. Shortly thereafter missions of several denominations got together and decided on a division of the country to avoid an overlap in their work. Kangwon became Methodist territory, and Henry moved to Syenchun Station, which was next on the list for a new man.

When some of the well-established missionaries didn't want to move just because another denomination was assigned the tract in which they were located, they simply changed denominations. They felt the differences weren't all that important. Years later when Mother was in the States giving a talk in a Methodist church, she explained the musical-chairs situation, telling of a Presbyterian woman who became a Methodist so she could stay where she was.

"Oh, how wonderful!" a woman sitting on the front row murmured under her breath.

"Several Methodist missionaries found themselves in Presbyterian territory," Mother continued, "so they too switched."

"Oh, how could they!" the same person said with a sigh.

"Pyuktong, Changsung, Sakchu, and Weiju are counties on the south shore of the Yalu River that separates Korea from Manchuria," Dr. Sharrocks said to Henry. "The area is mountainous, with few roads, many remote villages, and bitterly cold winters. It's the largest territory we assign to one man. Are you willing to accept the challenge?"

"I requested your hardest job, and I'll gladly take it," answered the young man, sitting a little straighter with a look of determination on his face.

Daddy takes a wife.

As promised, Henry returned to Ponca, Nebraska, to marry Ruth and brought his bride to their new home. For three years they shared a house with the Ross family until theirs could be built.

Missionaries in the early 1900s did all kinds of things for which they had no training. Henry earned a college degree and graduated from seminary without ever constructing so much as a chicken coop. Needing a house for his family in Syenchun, he built one.

The land in the mission compound assigned to the Lampes was on a hillside, where a large area had been leveled. For years Ruth collected the bits of tile that kept working their way to the surface and sent them to the curator of the museum in Seoul. Later investigation indicated that this had been the site of a granary in use about the time of Israel's King David.

Korean workers made bricks and roofing tiles and baked them in a kiln set up on site, and a hired Chinese contractor did the work. Toward the end of that time Ruth was expecting her second child and wasn't able to make a number of changes she would have liked. It was considered unseemly for a woman in her condition to appear in public. Willard arrived before the house was finished, but for years she regretted not having nice deep window sills.

"Today my wife had a fine, healthy son." Henry announced the good news to the contractor.

"Last year one boy," the grinning Chinese responded. "This year one boy, every year one boy. By and by plenty."

While exploring the hill behind the house, Henry discovered a spring gushing from the ground. It was good, pure water because there was nothing around to contaminate it. He had a well dug and pipes laid to the house, providing an abundant supply of the most wonderful soft water.

Over the next few years they planted gardens and harvested apples from their own trees. Spreading grapevines produced wonderful fruit, and every two years or so Ruth produced another baby.

Willard and Heydon

The house that Daddy built

Thirty years later

Cordelia, Willard, and Heydon

And Then There Were Ten

And God blessed them; and God said to them,
"Be fruitful and multiply."
Gen. 2:28a

"We want a girl," I shouted as I jumped up and down on that freezing January morning in 1927. Little puffs of vapor accompanied each word. "No, no," the boys objected, "we want a boy!"

All seven of us, four boys on one side of the porch and three girls on the other, loudly cast our votes for the sex of the child soon to be born. Because our station doctor was on a year's furlough, our parents were going to Seoul several weeks before the baby was due.

Mother gave each of us a hug and a kiss, urging us back into the house. We watched them from the bedroom window, our faces pressed against the cold glass. The cobblestone path down the hill to the main road was slippery, and Mother moved carefully, holding on to her husband's arm. They had a two-mile walk through town to the station. Heydon, Willard, and Cordelia had come home for Christmas vacation from Pyeng Yang Foreign School, a mission boarding school 150 miles to the south and were going back on the same train that Mother and Daddy would take all the way to Seoul. We four younger ones, Nathan, Betty, Jim, and

I watched the procession until they passed out of sight.

I churned with a mixture of distress and excitement. The thought of a new baby was wonderful, but Mother would be gone a long time. I loved to hug her. She was warm and soft and had a certain fragrance, uniquely hers, that I associated with comfort and security. Three whole months seemed forever to my six-year-old mind. Yes, I was sad.

But Aunt Hally, Hally Covington, one of the "single ladies" in the station, would be staying with us, and that made things okay! She was very fat, jolly, and lots of fun. She had a round, friendly face and a hairdo that intrigued me. It wound up in a small bun at the back of her head, but on the way there it waved in little ridges that went from one side to the other. I couldn't quite figure it out, but she must have done it with a curling iron.

Aunt Hally laughed a lot. Sometimes she laughed so hard she shook all over, and tears ran down her cheeks. She understood small children, too. Every once in a while she'd have a dinner party just for us with no grown-ups invited. We had the best things to eat, stuff you could pick up with your fingers. Dessert was vanilla ice cream with lots of hot chocolate sauce that we put on ourselves. She never told us when to stop. When I couldn't eat all of mine, she wrapped up the hardened chocolate in wax paper to take home.

Aunt Hally didn't like spinach or rutabagas. She ordered the meals while Mother was away, so we didn't have to eat them either, nor did we have to have lessons because she taught at the Po Sung Girls' School every day. We were going to have a nice long vacation.

On February 12, 1927, Molly was born, a beautiful ten-pound-fourteen-ounce girl! Now we were even at four boys and four girls and were the largest Presbyterian missionary family in Korea—in the whole wide world. Pyeng Yang Foreign School had children from three other mission families, each boasting seven of them. When word came that the Lampes had moved into the lead with an eighth child, the Talmages, Wilsons, and Newlands stopped speaking to them.

We got along fine at home until I caught a cold that settled in my ear. Today an abscessed ear would be no big deal, but that was before sulfa drugs and penicillin came on the scene. The most potent drug at that time was aspirin. I ran a high fever, and the mission doctor was not in country. Poor Aunt Hally was desperate. There was no immediate way to contact my parents, so she took the advice of a Korean doctor who thought an operation was in order. He not only cleaned out the abscess but also opened up the ear from below the lobe, leaving a one-inch scar on my jaw. When Mother heard of it, she was furious.

Because of the lingering infection, I was not permitted out of the house in the bitter cold. As the others bundled up to slide down the hill on their Flexible Flyers, I could only watch from the big front window, my head swathed in bandages. The bad part was a daily visit from the doctor, who changed the dressing. I'm sure he tried to be gentle, but it hurt terribly. Although I was a small child, it took several of them to hold me down.

"Can't I sit on your lap while he does it?" I begged Mother on her first day back.

"Precious little girl," she soothed as she gently lifted me, "let me give you a hug. I know it hurts, and my tummy still hurts, too. Try to sit very quietly, and it will be over in a minute."

"Okay," I answered as she nuzzled my neck in the way I loved. I didn't struggle or pull away, and it was over quickly, just as she said it would be. The best part was snuggling against her, aware of her special fragrance, wrapped in the safety of her arms. It was a good ending to a bitter winter. Babies are fantastic, but best of all, Mother and Daddy were home at last. Our family was complete.

It was so nice to have a baby sister.

On the first really warm day of spring, the doctor took off the heavy bandages that swathed most of my head and covered the incision with a Band-Aid. It was the first day of knee-socks, too (because the temperature got all the way up to sixty), and I was allowed outdoors wearing only a light sweater. The sap in the maple trees was beginning to run, making sweet icicles that we enjoyed sucking first thing in the morning before they melted. The ground was wet and cold, but iris shoots poked up on both sides of the cobblestone walkway. Leaf buds were ready to burst, the birds were busy gathering twigs, and the sky was a brilliant blue. The whole world seemed wonderful—and it was grand to have a new little sister.

Early Itineration

How lovely on the mountains are the feet of him who brings good news,
Who announces peace and brings good news of happiness
Who announces salvation,
and says to Zion, "Your God reigns!"
Is. 52:7

Soon after his arrival in Syenchun, Daddy had his first experience "itinerating" the countryside with Dr. Ross, a seasoned missionary.

I remember Dr. Ross as being the exact size and shape of Santa Claus. He had little wisps of white hair on his mostly bald head, a happy face, and merry blue eyes behind rimless glasses. He even had a nice round belly just like pictures of Santa. One of the things I particularly liked about him was that when we'd dance the Virginia Reel after station dinners, he always told me I was his favorite partner. He'd come to stand in front of me and offering his hand say, "May I have this dance, Miss Lampe?"

Dr. Ross and Daddy started out on their circuit with four horses, one for each to ride, and one apiece for baggage.

Daddy preferred to walk—he held the record for the mile in the Midwest for years—and after the first two days sent his riding horse back. As time passed he graduated to a bike with a horse for baggage and then to a car. Right up to the end of his stay in 1940, however, there were places that couldn't be reached except on foot. He often covered up to forty miles a day. Many a time he arrived at a remote village or mountaintop hamlet, absolutely sure that in such an isolated place there would be no Western influence. To his amazement he'd find hand-turned and treadle Singer sewing machines.

"My, how I admire those Singer salesmen," he remarked one day. "They know they have a good product and are marvels at selling it. They're a good example for me with the best news in the world to share—that Jesus is Lord."

There were no hotels or inns worthy of the name, so in those early days each traveler took along everything he needed. Daddy's trips usually lasted from a month to six weeks. It was customary for the missionaries to stay with church members. Nevertheless, he took along a folding camp cot and bedroll, a small trunk of clothing and personal items, a store of food, pots and pans, a camp stove, Bibles, hymn books, and tracts. A Korean was hired to assist with the baggage, take care of the ponies, and do the cooking. Daddy felt that lugging around all that paraphernalia was too cumbersome but went along with it at first.

"I learned to eat and drink little during the evening meal while in the country," Daddy later said when reminiscing about living in a typical Korean home. "In the middle of the night it's a long dark walk to the facility (an open trench with two boards on which to stand or squat and a box of paper nearby—usually newsprint). My hosts always provided a brass *au-gong* (chamber pot), but I didn't use it unless absolutely necessary. I liked to spare their wives the chore of cleaning it up."

"I was usually given the room at the end of a three-room house, away from the kitchen, and the rest of the family occupied the middle one. I very much appreciated the privacy, and since I didn't sleep on the floor, it was better for the family to have the warmer place.

"I'm an early riser, but a Korean wife was always up long before me, and my room began to warm with the fire she built for cooking the breakfast rice. Hot air and smoke from the fire warmed the stone flooring as they passed through a duct from the kitchen to the third room, then up the chimney."

All went well until a stay in Sin Weiju when Daddy lodged with a church elder who was a prosperous dry-goods merchant. He was given space in the main house with the family while his helper slept in a storeroom next door. The Korean Church taught that Sunday was a day of rest and worship and not for taking care of business. Daddy was surprised to see his host spending long hours in the storeroom Sunday afternoon and evening, counting money. He didn't say anything, but he was curious about the unusual practice. Likewise, the host seemed a bit distracted and distant—rather quiet. As Daddy was ready to depart, his host took him aside. "Please, Pastor Lampe, do not bring this helper with you again," That was all, but upon returning to Syenchun, Daddy received a letter of apology. The elder wrote: "I'm sorry for seeming so concerned with money on Sunday. I was checking the collection. Another elder gave it to me after church, noting the amount. When I made the count, it was far short. Later I discovered that a number of cured animal skins hanging in my storeroom were missing. I'm afraid your helper is responsible. He was the only one with the opportunity. I don't want you to make a big deal of it, but I thought you should know."

Daddy felt sick about it and offered to make restitution. The elder allowed him to repay the missing collection money, for many in the congregation were poor, but he took the loss on the skins. Daddy dismissed the helper. Nothing was said about the theft, but he was sure the man understood that he knew.

From then on Daddy determined to break with tradition; he ate all his food with the host families. He couldn't face endless breakfasts of rice, fish soup, and *kimchi*, a hot, spicy side dish made of cabbage or turnips, garlic, salt, and red pepper, so he carried a tin of rolled oats and a jar of instant Postum, both of which he could prepare himself. Daddy said the reason Scotsmen and English horses were so fine was that they ate oats. He also learned to suck raw eggs and enjoyed a couple of them every morning.

Additionally, Mother saw to it that he had a supply of beaten biscuits for snacks. They were a homemade version of soda crackers that we had before we could get the store-bought kind. Daddy never got sick while away. I don't remember his ever being sick. He was a remarkably healthy, happy man.

Sanitation in the Korean home was a problem. Bathing had to be accomplished in a public bathhouse if there was one. Once a house was infested with vermin it was next to impossible to get rid of them, and they were very easy for a guest to acquire. When Daddy returned from a trip, Mother made sure his bedroll and all of his clothes were hung on the laundry line in the back yard and assiduously inspected before they were permitted inside. No bedbugs or lice in her house, thank you very much!

At the age of twelve we went off to the missionary boarding school in Pyeng Yang. When Mother and Daddy came for a visit and stayed with the Phillips, Mrs. Phillips invited us younger Lampes to come for dinner. We were happy to have a reprieve from dorm food, and it was a treat to spend some time with our parents.

No one could ever say that life in the mission field was dull because there were so many interesting people, and Ma Phil was one of them. She was known for her strong opinions on most subjects, and she had no hesitation in voicing them. Like my father, Pa Phil was an itinerant preacher, so at dinner they were soon swapping stories.

"Do you mean to tell me, Henry, that you actually eat their food when you're up country?" he asked. "I take everything with me, and I'm surprised to hear you don't."

"I gave that up years ago when my helper helped himself to some of my host's property and a good portion of the Sunday collection! For me, living on the land's been an excellent experience," he answered, "and I don't regret the change at all. I have been blessed with good health, and I'll tell you this; if you ever get any bad food, that kimchi will burn it right out of you."

Ma Phil was all for the traditional ways and would have none

Hostess

But a lover of hospitality
Titus 1:8

Mother loved people. She wanted to know all about them and made them feel welcome and appreciated. She arranged parties at the drop of a hat, serving ice cream in soup bowls so you'd be sure to have enough. She herself had been served a generous portion of life's gusto.

In the last few years of her life she had a series of strokes and heart attacks that required numerous hospital stays. In a few days she knew the names of all the nurses who attended her, knew all about their families, the names of their children, how old they were, and how they were doing.

A little on the short side compared to the rest of us, she was plump but not fat, just right for hugging. Her light brown hair was parted on the side and pulled back into a bun at the nape of her neck, and blue eyes sparkled behind her glasses. She smiled easily and loved to tell a story. Though a woman of many talents, fortunately for the rest of us she wasn't a perfectionist. Her good-humored tolerance extended to her own affairs as well as ours, typically demonstrated when she was finishing up an embroidered table runner and not too pleased with some of her work. Smoothing it out she remarked, "Oh well, nobody's going to notice a few uneven stitches on the back of a galloping horse!"

As a missionary wife and mother, she was a tremendous asset. Daddy was the quiet one of the family, but she never diminished him in any way. She was proud of him. I watched as she introduced herself to a new man just arrived from the States.

"My husband is that good-looking fellow standing by the piano," she said, pointing to him. Her antenna was always out, probing every situation, making contact and interacting with those who came into her sphere of influence.

Syenchun was a small city without benefit of good hotels or restaurants. Sure, there were the *yag-wons* (Korean inns) and an assortment of noodle shops, but nothing that looked particularly inviting to foreigners. Not infrequently Mother encountered people in the market who were obviously from another land, engaged them in conversation, and invited them home for dinner. One day she met an American Catholic priest downtown. In 1917 during the days of very slow transportation, years and years went by before any of them could get home to see their families. Some expected never to go back at all.

"I imagine it's been some time since you've had a home-cooked dinner. If you're free, come have supper with us," she invited after talking to Father Paul.

"Oh, my dear lady, that would be like a gift from heaven. I'll be delighted to come. Just tell me where and when."

"Fine. We'll see you at six o'clock," she said, giving him directions. There was plenty of time to kill the fatted calf. The poor fellow had probably eaten nothing but Korean food for months and was aching for something that tasted familiar. Father Paul showed up right on time and of course was wearing clerical dress with his rosary and crucifix. Our missionaries wore regular shirts, for in that era a Protestant minister would rather die than be mistaken for a Catholic priest.

Cordelia was fascinated with the guest's appearance and in no time was sitting on his lap. Mother went to the kitchen to check on dinner and when she returned found Father Paul on all fours with the three-year-old on his back using the rosary as reins. Heydon and Willard shouted, "Gittie up, horsie!" as he charged around the dining room table.

Dinner that night was roast chicken with dressing and gravy, rice, vegetables, waldorf salad (with peanuts—you couldn't get walnuts), biscuits, butter, and jam. Father Paul was offered second and third helpings, and he kept wolfing it down. When the dishes were cleared away and the apple pie with ice cream arrived, he put a hand on his stomach and groaned.

"There is no way I can take another bite, but I simply can't pass up such a treat," he said. "May I go outside for a while to make room for it?" My parents laughed and agreed, so out he went with Heydon and Willard in tow, running circles around the house until he could face dessert.

Our house was well suited for station dinners. The living and dining rooms were combined from the front to back. When the dining table was extended as far as it would go and boards set on sawhorses were covered with pads and tablecloths, it could seat thirty with ease. The younger children usually ate together at card tables.

Nathan, a serious little fellow of four, had been avidly absorbing the grammar instruction that went on during family mealtime. To reinforce the function of a preposition, the case in point was *out.* It began with "Keep out," with the "out" strongly emphasized. As the illustrations continued, everybody adding his bit, it became "Keep out of my business," then "Keep your nose out of my business," and finally "Keep your dirty old nose out of my business." While a mission board member from the States was holding forth during a station dinner, Nathan, dressed in pajamas and wanting to make an impression on the guest, opened the door and looked straight at him.

"Keep your dirty old nose out of my business!" he said in a commanding voice. He was so pleased with himself that he gave everyone a big smile before scampering off to bed. Poor Mother! She tried, but no amount of explaining was going to fix that one.

Lexie, our fox terrier, was a dear and precious member of the family. About twice a year she produced a litter. She was a fierce little mother, and no one could get near her basket for several days after she gave birth. Mother made sure she had plenty of food and water, but none of us was allowed to get near the pups until she went outside. The doors between Lexie's basket and the back door were left open a crack so she could go out when she needed to.

On the occasion of another station dinner, the honored guest was in the midst of expounding on board policy when one of us whispered rather loudly, "Mother, Lexie just went outdoors." Two days earlier she had brought forth a whole bunch of pups, and we were eager to get a good close look at them. Someone else heard the whisper and repeated it. The startled guest looked on as everybody jumped up from the table and rushed into the bedroom to count the newcomers. We didn't mean to be rude, but in Syenchun the arrival of Lexie's pups was an event!

In their retirement years, Mother and Daddy lived in Iowa City, and their three-bedroom house always had room for any who came. They shopped moving sales to find beds that would come apart and store easily. When we arrived for a visit we set them up. We knew where to find the linens and blankets.

The house at 810 Otto Street was always open to Korean students at the University of Iowa; it became their home away from home. They missed their native cooking, too, and frequently brought along the makings to prepare a feast. It was no wonder then that in 1955 Mother received an award we all felt she richly deserved. She was named Iowa Mother of the Year.

Our Daily Bread

. . . but bring them up in the nurture and admonitions of the Lord.
Eph. 6:4

Vacations are wonderful and all sorts of trips are fun, but the greatest satisfaction of life comes from things accomplished in a steady, routine sort of way. I grew to realize how true that is when I came to understand the way Mother organized family life in the beautiful but primitive Korean setting. With eight children to rear in addition to the care of dogs, cats, birds, goldfish, chickens, and cows, she had a very full plate. She oversaw the growing, canning, and storage of most of our food. There was bread to bake; clothing to make and mend; children to love, discipline, nurse, and teach the three R's. When she found flowers growing wild on *Tai-mok San,* she had the outside man transplant yellow, white, and purple iris along the walk and lilies of the valley in the flower bed under Daddy's study window. Through it all, Mother was in her glory.

My debut

During furlough years, she was in great demand as a speaker for women's groups. She invited questions and comments.

"You really do have an easy life with all kinds of servants in your home—a cook, cook's helper, laundry woman, sewing woman, and outside man. We can't afford all that," said a listener.

Mother's answer was right to the point. "You have servants, too. Somebody teaches your children in school. Others deliver your milk every morning, bake your bread, process your food, make your clothes, sweep your streets, and take away the garbage." The audience agreed.

It was a tall order, but Ruth Lampe was an organizer. Never far from hand was her list of things to do. As each task was completed, she marked it off with a big flourish.

"While the rest of the ladies are thinking of how they are going to do something, Ruth has it done," Daddy commented a number of times. He was proud of her, too.

I think Mother and Daddy must have been ideal Christian parents. They loved each other, and they let each of us know that we had some special gift, unique and cherished.

Heydon was the eldest and always a responsible person. He was tall and handsome with happy blue eyes. Like most of us he had the fair wavy hair inherited from our father.

We counted on quick-witted Willard to be in one kind of mischief or another. He was tall, too, of slender build, and had a way with the girls.

Cordelia was the first girl, a striking blonde with wide-set blue eyes and a trim figure. Like her brother, she was often in hot water because she didn't hesitate to challenge authority. In boarding school she regarded every rule as one to be broken. Her full name, Helen Cordelia, gradually evolved into the affectionate nickname of "Hunkey." We didn't know it was considered a bad word until we came to the States. Our Hunkey was special, a much-loved sister.

Nathan was a serious fellow of average height. When he was little, he was a favorite of the Korean staff, who called him *Nung-gam* (old man), which was as close as they could come to pronouncing his name. They taught him to mimic an elderly Korean gentleman by stroking his chin as if he had a beard and say in a deep voice, "Ah'hum, ah'hum."

Betty was a voracious reader and a great student. She had an easygoing, sweet disposition, and everybody loved her. A born homemaker, she liked to cook, sew, and embroider. Not my bag at all. I was too much of a tomboy.

I'm the little one in front.

I came next and was a reluctant dragon. The whole family missed summer at the beach because of me, and poor Mother suffered mightly with the heat. The due date came and went and still no baby. Finally the doctor helped mother nature along with a forceps delivery. I was bald as a billiard ball until the age of two. When I did get hair it broke the pattern—straight as a stick and platinum blond. I was skinny and sickly, and crooked teeth meant I couldn't chew my food properly. That I had a hard time sitting still must have been a trial to Mother during lessons. I longed only for recess.

Next to the last was Jim, who had a very active imagination. He was most like Willard in looks and disposition, growing into a handsome man and one of the kindest you'd ever want to meet.

Molly, the baby of the family, was the pet of all except Jim. When very young they developed a strong sibling rivalry that was a constant cause for correction. One day when she was looking at a family picture taken before she was born she asked, "Where was I?" Jim was quick to answer with great scorn, "You were just dirt. We kept you in a box on the front steps, and every time I went by it, I gave it a hard kick."

In the States before Molly was born

Molly had a disposition like Betty's and was favored by all the servants. When Kang-sie made cinnamon rolls Sunday mornings and scraped the extra sweet from the bottom of the pan, she'd always give it to Molly. While we were having family worship in the morning, Kang-sie went into the bedroom and made Molly's bed. That was a chore required of each of us.

"You must let Molly try," Mother told her. "How will she ever learn if you keep doing it for her?"

"Oh, but she is so little!" The answer was always the same.

As a child I was frail and puny, but Mother always found something complimentary to say—I had such a nice, straight little nose and that she loved the way my pink and coral ears lay close to my head. She never mentioned that I needed braces or my straight hair and miserably thin fingernails. Bless her.

Nathan, Jim, and I had malaria all during our childhood. Other problems such as a bad cold caused it to flare up with its high fever, chills, and sweats. We had to take quinine year round, and it made our ears ring.

Family portrait in 1926

Life wasn't easy, but it was a joy. Mother said the only thing she would consider a missionary hardship was sending us so far from home when it was time for us to attend college in the States.

Answers to letters took two months if the response was made immediately. Many a time I'd hear Mother and Daddy agonize over one or another of the older children who was facing a difficult situation without their being present to give guidance and encouragement. Mother had a Sunday School class for women in the Korean church and taught sewing and embroidery in the Po Sung Girls' School, but her chief occupation was her family.

We had a fixed daily routine that never varied, even during vacations. Except at the beach, where it could have disturbed the neighbors, a handbell announced our six-thirty rising time. Betty and I shared a room right over our parents', so if Mother didn't hear us moving around, she rapped the back of her hairbrush on the hot-air pipe. It was loud enough to wake the dead, but we had to call out to let her know we were up.

Breakfast was at seven o'clock. I was frequently the last to appear because I had trouble dressing. High-buttoned shoes and that blasted buttonhook were hard to manage, and the pantywaist with the straps that held up long lisle stockings seemed to take forever to straighten out. After waiting for me to arrive for the blessing Daddy announced, "Here comes the late Miss Lampe." That was his only reproof, but it was enough to make me determine never to be late again—until the next morning.

Breakfast was fresh fruit, cooked cereal with milk and salt (no sugar), and toast with butter. We usually had apples that Daddy grew. He had a special friend in Manchuria who was planting apple trees from seed all over the country. Any that were undamaged we'd save for him. When there were enough dried seeds, Daddy sent them to "Mr. Johnny Appleseed" in Manchuria. The fantastic fruit we get from South Korea today came originally from just such trees grown from a happenstance seed.

Collecting the uncut seeds on our plates, we counted them with

> One I love, two I love, three I love I say,
> Four I love with all my heart,
> And five I cast away.

Six he loves,
Seven she loves,
Eight they both love.
Nine they quarrel,
Ten they part,
Eleven they die of a broken heart.

At seven-thirty we had family worship, or in Korean, *kito*. Daddy read a chapter from the Bible; we memorized a verse and repeated a previously learned passage or a psalm. Next we repeated the one we had just memorized and a chapter in the series we had learned. Before leaving home all of us had committed to memory nearly one hundred psalms and chapters and the shorter catechism. Daddy consulted both the Korean and the mission prayer calendars for the people we were to pray for that day; then on our knees he led us in the Lord's Prayer.

Following *kito* came one of the best times of all. Mother and Daddy kissed each other and each of us. Sometimes we'd try to kiss them first, but they held us at arm's length until they had kissed each other. It was sort of a game.

Next, one of us was asked to get the candy kept in Daddy's study closet, high up on a shelf. There were other interesting things in there such as his .22 rifle, but we weren't allowed to touch any of it. Only if he asked us to get something could we go near his desk or that closet. The candy box was ceremoniously presented, and we were permitted to take one piece whether large or small.

The five-pound box of Fanny May or Busy Bee Christmas candy Uncle Willard sent yearly was a special treat. When we had a visitor from the States staying with us for a few days, a box of it was inadvertently left on a table in the living room. We kids dashed off, Mother headed for the kitchen, and Daddy went into his study to meet a caller. The guest found a book and sat down to read right next to the candy. While thus occupied he mindlessly consumed a whole layer. Somebody put the box away, but the next day (the guest having departed), Mother was furious. How could somebody who should know better have been so thoughtless!

With teeth brushed and beds made, we were ready for lessons at eight. The schoolroom was on the second floor at the rear of the house. Bookshelves about three feet high lined the back wall with windows above. Pictures of Washington and Lincoln hung on one wall, the American flag on another, and a blackboard on the fourth. We did daily assignments from the Calvert Correspondence Course.

A half-hour recess started at ten o'clock with a glass of milk. One day our delight in an extra long one turned to sadness. Our wonderful black cat was dead. We first called her Felix but after discovering she was a girl had to change it to Felicia. She was a lovely pet, frisky and full of fun, but she developed a penchant for killing a neighbor's chickens at night.

Mother read everything she could find about how to break animals of bad habits, but nothing worked. One suggested remedy was to tie the head of a chicken around the cat's neck. She tried it, but Felicia kept on killing chickens, so she had to be destroyed.

Mother was very practical. She loved the cat too, but it couldn't be broken of its bad habit. There was a price to be paid by us and Felicia. I began to see that even in our perfect world there was sadness and death.

Because there were no veterinary services of any kind, all such matters you had to take care of yourself. Without our knowledge, she had Tin Hoop-i, the outside man, fill a big *toke* (earthenware jar), with water.

"I gave Felicia one last hug, then put her into a gunny sack with a heavy stone in it, tied the top shut, and dropped it into the water. There was a scratch or two on the side and all was quiet. I was terribly sorry to do this, but I had no choice," Mother told us later. She helped us understand.

Tin Hoop-i made a little coffin for her, but when he nailed down the lid the tip of her ear stuck out, which we thought was really quite exciting if not downright spooky. We all touched it to see what a dead cat felt like. After school that day we were allowed to have a funeral for Felicia, carried out with the full Korean ritual of wailing and crying as we carried the little box up the hill to the cemetery. There her tiny grave, marked with a wooden cross, was placed between those of two missionaries.

Dr. Tipton, one of the early physicians in Syenchun, insisted that the women's mental health and general well-being was vital to the happiness of the community. Having been with little people all day, they deserved some time without them underfoot. They also needed exercise. So every afternoon the mothers went for a walk, but no kids could go along. No amount of teasing or pestering would avail. They were gone about an hour and returned refreshed and glad to see us.

After dinner came story time. Mother read aloud from books that we took turns choosing. Jim was fascinated by *Little Black Sambo,* a boy who ate 169 pancakes all by himself. Fantastic! When we were old enough to enjoy them, we graduated to classics such as *Tom Sawyer, Huck Finn,* and *A Tale of Two Cities* as well as stories from the *Saturday Evening Post..* The *Post* came every week and was one of Mother's favorite magazines. We never missed sharing serialized chapters of *Tugboat Annie* and could hardly wait for the next issue to arrive. Mother liked to say, "Anyone can live happily with the Bible, Montgomery Ward's catalog (Sears was not available in Korea), and the *Saturday Evening Post.*"

Mother loved to have her hair brushed and combed. If one of us stood behind her chair and brushed with firm, gentle strokes, we'd get an extra story. "That feels so good," she said. "When I get to Heaven I'm going to ask that a little cherub be assigned to do nothing but brush my hair." I wonder who that little one is.

Eight o'clock was bedtime for the younger ones; Mother and Daddy read aloud or to themselves until they, too, went to bed at ten. Like clockwork, the Lampe family's schedule was predictable and comfortable.

Traditions

. . . and hold the traditions which you have been taught . . .
II Thess. 2:15

We made candy or cookies every Sunday afternoon when the servants were out, and there was always a smell of popcorn in the house when we got back from church in one of the station homes. For dinner we had roast chicken with all the trimmings and apple pie for desert. In the evening we read Bible stories and played games while we ate bowl after bowl of that lovely buttered, salted popcorn.

On the l7th of September, Willard's birthday, we harvested the big *chat namoo* (pine tree) in our front yard. We shook down the huge cones and removed a nut from under each petal. They had to be cracked and the nutmeats stored in glass jars. Our favorite use of them was for flavoring in vanilla ice cream.

In the fall one or two pigs that had been fattening for several months were taken downtown to be slaughtered. When they were returned to the house on bull carts, Tin-Hoop-i and another man hung them by the hind legs from a beam in the laundry room, the only basement room with a cement floor. Mother and Daddy put on long white aprons and with huge knives and cleavers cut up pork for the year. The yield was head cheese, scrapple, chops, and roasts. The smokehouse bulged with hams and bacons to be cured. If we stayed out of the way, we children were invited to watch all this exciting activity. "The inside of a pig is much like ours, so it will be a fine lesson in biology," Mother said.

As each organ was removed, Daddy kept up a running commentary. "Now this is like your heart that pumps your blood, and this," holding it in his hands, "is like your stomach where your food goes after it's swallowed. Remember how we constantly remind you to take small bites and chew them well? Your stomach likes that a lot. The dark brown shiny thing is the liver, and look at this small balloon over here. It holds bile that helps digest food. The liver is a very efficient chemical factory that keeps things going for us. These two little things are kidneys. They clean a lot of bad stuff out of our blood that could make us sick. They do a wonderful job. The Lord gave us two of them, so if one gets sick the other can still keep us healthy."

Finding out how all the parts worked together and were so well packaged in exactly the right place was quite marvelous. I was growing curious about my own body and wondered if I'd ever be like Hunkey, who was beginning to have little bumps on her chest. She was seven years older than I, but I was impatient.

"You won't have to carry a lamp up to bed any more," Mother remarked when electricity arrived in the early 1930s. "With just a push on the switch a light will go on. There will be one in every room, so we'll have no more kerosene smell or dripping wax."

Day after day workmen toiled to run the wires along the baseboards, up the walls, and across the ceilings where the light fixtures hung. Looking like miniature railroad tracks, two black wires were separated every foot or so by porcelain insulators. We delighted in such modern luxury in spite of lacking adequate power. When a second or third light turned on, all the rest dimmed a little. We continued to cook and heat with a wood-burning stove and furnace. Our kitchen never boasted a refrigerator, though some families in Seoul and Pyeng Yang had them.

Ice for the whole year came from the Kagle River, which ran through town. When it froze several feet thick behind the dam near the Sung Sill Academy, the mission boys' school, it was cut into nine-cubic-foot blocks, loaded on a cart, and brought to the house. Men hired for the job clamped huge ice tongs on one block at a time and ran a pole through the loops at the end of the tongs. Resting the pole on his shoulders, each carrier steadied the ice with one hand and grasped the pole with the other to tote it up the hill to the ice-house. Inside was a pit about fifteen feet deep and of the same width and length whose sides and bottom were lined with granite. It was protected by a tin roof and shaded by trees. At the start of winter it was cleaned out and left open to a hard freeze before the ice was delivered.

Ice delivered to our back yard

"Huggi-dong, huggie-dong cha."

The men wore straw sandals over padded socks to keep from slipping on the steep footpath. As they lifted their loads and started up the hill, they kept in step with a sing-song chant. The first man sang out, *huggi-dong*. The second man responded with *huggi-dong cha,* and so it went all the way to the top. They stacked the blocks into one huge, solid cube and covered its sides and top with *kay* (rice chaff). It would last until the next winter, supplying the icebox and making ice cream possible even in the hottest weather.

First thing on a winter morning Daddy took his flashlight to the garage to check a thermometer mounted on the north wall.

"Well, what's the temperature? Ruth, you guess first," he said as we began breakfast. Sometimes frost on the inside of the windows made beautiful patterns on the glass, and water in the bedroom pitchers froze solid. On such mornings, Kangsi brought hot water from the kitchen for us to wash with. Shivering and shaking, we found it particularly hard to get out of bed, regardless of the threat of being late.

During January and February the temperature usually dropped to around zero to minus ten degrees F. One morning it was colder than usual.

"It might be best to keep the children inside for a while," Daddy said as he came in. "Wait until it warms up a bit before they go out to play. It's minus thirty-four."

In the early spring when the snow and ice were melting and the streams full of clear, cold water, Mrs. Ross took us on long walks to gather pussy willows. She looked quite different from the other women in the station. Her dresses were always dark, with high collars and long sleeves, and her skirts went all the way to the floor. Strangest of all, she wore high-buttoned shoes, something I never could understand. The greatest graduation in my whole life was getting out of those miserable things and wearing shoes that tied or buckled. But she was wonderful the way she carefully showed us where to find hepaticas, violets, and *hal-muni got* (grandmother flowers), the fuzzy, gray, bell-shaped flowers with red centers. They were so soft and fragile. Mrs. Ross may have been different, but I certainly did like to dance the Virginia Reel with her husband!

When the first strawberry blossoms appeared, we were permitted to wear bobby socks; and when the first ripe strawberry was discovered, we could go barefoot. What bliss! We ran outdoors to wriggle our toes in the dirt. I'm told that when Willard was small and couldn't wait for the strawberries to ripen, he picked the largest one he could find and painted it red. I don't know whether he got away with it , but I doubt it.

Being a Nebraska girl, Mother felt we should have the experience of planting and tending a garden. Each of us was responsible for one kind of flower and one vegetable or fruit. I figured I wasn't much of a farmer, so I chose the easiest ones, nasturtiums, grown on either side of the front steps. After the seeds were well sprouted, Tin-hoop-i gave me little pegs and helped me pound them into the ground by each seedling. We ran a stout string from the peg to a nail driven into the frame of the screen above. The wonderful thing about nasturtiums is that they grow fast. In a couple of weeks those little shoots seemed to twist and climb up that string right before my eyes. I felt that God and I had a fine partnership. Together we produced some beautiful flowers for the table. It was a happy day when I discovered there was nectar at the bottom of each blossom's little stem.

My vegetable was the radish, grown in the back yard next to the lettuce. I didn't have to wait forever before I could pull some and take them to Kangsi to put in the salad. I liked radishes and thought mine were especially good.

Nathan had a strawberry bed that yielded very large Rocky Mountain Reds so mild that nobody got a rash from eating them. One day he brought in a huge one, whose circumference was seven inches by tape measure. Nathan was very proud that day.

Daddy's hobby was growing apple trees: King Davids, Johnathans, Yellow Stark Delicious, Rome Beauties, and Bellflowers. The latter were especially big and light yellow in color with little black speckles. When picked at exactly the right time, they were the best. If there was a bumper crop of Bellflowers, the limbs had to be propped up so they wouldn't break. Because there were so many, a count was made on a single tree so we could estimate the yield . One tree might produce over a thousand apples.

Each piece of fruit was carefully picked and handed to a person on the ground who wrapped it in paper and put it in a barrel. The first year Jim and I were permitted to help, Mother never failed to remind us to sit or stand on a good strong branch, hold on with one hand, and pick with the other. We shouted our agreement as we scrambled up to where we could reach the apples without breaking the branches and still be safe. Only perfect ones went into the barrels, but nothing was wasted. Any bruised or fallen ones we set aside for applesauce, apple butter, juice, jelly, stewing, and drying. Yes, we had apples!

Many events during the year were honored with a traditional ceremony that helped build a whole book of happy memories, but there were two occasions we did not enjoy that returned as faithfully as the seasons—spring and fall housecleaning. Everything, and I mean everything, was turned inside out, upside down, cleaned, polished, and put back. It was a two-week orgy, and in the process Mother took inventory, discarding some things, saving others.

"If you keep something for seven years you'll find a use for it," she swore, but she always had a list of items to be purchased when funds permitted.

At a station gathering one spring, Mother overheard a bitter complaint.

"The turmoil we have to suffer is a terror. I nearly go crazy until it's over. I don't understand why Katherine puts us through such an exercise twice every year," said Mr. Hoffman to my father.

"Well, I don't know," he answered. "Ruth doesn't seem to have much trouble with it." Big mistake! Mother always planned our upheavals during one of his extended trips, but after hearing that she decided to educate her husband. The next one took place when he was home.

"What in the world is going on, Ruth?" he asked. "Why are all of my books stacked on the floor? I can't find anything, and the rug in my study is gone and so are all the curtains!"

"Oh, just the usual spring cleaning, dear," she answered. "It will all be over in a couple of weeks. If you need something just let me know, and I'll find it for you." Thus Daddy learned first-hand what it was all about.

Every missionary family in Korea had to endure a semiannual deworming. Without indoor plumbing or running water in most homes, answers to nature's call were frequently accomplished at the side of the road or behind sheltering bushes. Though not malnourished, a large number of Korean babies had distended bellies, indicating the presence of roundworms. Indeed, most of the population was so infested. Dried feces powdered and became airborne, distributing the eggs across the land. Anything could be contaminated. Careful as we were to wash hands and food, we got worms anyway.

Grinding our teeth while we slept was apparently a sign of

their presence. When Mother heard it she thought, Uh-oh, time to order the santnin. The horrible-tasting stuff came in powder form, each dose in its own little folded paper. For three nights in a row before bed, she lined us up and made us take it. First she put a little jelly in a tablespoon, shook the santnin on top, then covered it with a little more jelly. No matter how she disguised it, we still gagged and could hardly get it down.

"Thanks, Mother, but I don't need any jelly on top," said Willard, taking the spoon from her hand. As soon as she wasn't looking he blew off as much of the powder as he could before popping the spoon in his mouth. We didn't say a thing. We just wished we could have been so clever.

Twenty-four hours after the last dose came the Epsom salts purge. It wasn't fun either, but Mother told us, "Hold your breath while you drink it, then have some water, and you'll never taste it." It was true; we didn't. For the next two days we used a chamber pot rather than the toilet so Mother could inspect the results. Always positive.

Years later when I was married and had a family, the Caltex Oil Company for whom my husband worked, assigned my husband a three-year tour in Korea. After only seven months we were evacuated from Seoul at the beginning of the war in 1950. Upon our return to the States, they requested that the whole family get complete physicals.

"It might be a good idea to have stool examinations for roundworms," I suggested to the physician and explained that my young children had more than likely picked them up.

"I don't wish anything like that on you," the doctor said, "but we'll have a look. We hardly ever see those things here." When we received the test results, everything was negative.

About a week later Jimmy called, "Mommie, come wipe my tail fedders." By the time I reached the bathroom he was off of the toilet and bent over, ready for the cleanup. What a sight greeted my eyes. There, hanging out of his little bottom were three inches of wiggling roundworm! I carefully pulled out all six inches of it

Artisans

In all labor there is profit.
Prov. 14:23

Of all the itinerant Chinese merchants who visited us every spring and fall during the 1930s, the lace man was our favorite. Carrying two big bundles tied kitty-corner in dark blue cloth, one on each end of a bamboo pole across his shoulders, he arrived at the front door, asking, "Lady, you wan-chi lace?" The gentleman was always welcome.

Coming from north China, he traveled the length and breadth of the land by train, jitney, and on foot. Foreigners were his principal market. Except for a very few businessmen and government officials in Pyeng Yang, Seoul, and Pusan, American missionaries made up the big majority of them. Satisfied customers recommend him to friends in other towns and villages. Before long he had a network of shoppers scattered all over the country.

Ever the wise merchant, he stocked his inventory with goods to our taste and budget. We in Syenchun were fortunate to be just fifty miles south of the border and probably his first stop.

Mother served him tea before he spread a cloth on the living room floor and unpacked his precious merchandise, arranging it enticingly for all to see. We children were quickly dispatched to let everybody in the compound know of his arrival.

The news was magic. The four or five women who home-schooled their young came right away, clutching their purses, hoping to satisfy their shopping lists before the best things were snatched up. Miss Ingerson, the station nurse, couldn't make it until just before dinner, nor could Miss Stevens, the principal of Po Sung Girls' School. They always seemed happy with their purchases and never complained about getting stuck with the leftovers. Only mildly interested, the men came if they could. It was amusing to see them standing against the wall, arms crossed, chatting among themselves. Some kept a keen eye on what their wives were putting in a to-buy stack.

There were fabulous point Venice tablecloths, which we could not afford, and much less elaborate kinds we could. He had embroidered pillow cases and covers, table runners, dresser sets, delicate handkerchiefs, and lace by the yard. If the price was right all the girls in the family bought silk blouses decorated with embroidery and lace, every one a work of art and far superior to anything produced locally. Even though he protested our polite but hard bargaining, claiming we would reduce him to poverty, he always made a killing.

The china-mending man came as regularly as the lace man, and we couldn't have done without him. No matter how careful the servants were, cups, plates, and various fragile treasures got broken. Mother often cautioned Kang-si, the cook. "Please be more careful with the Haviland. It can't be replaced."

"Oh well, it's only cracked," Kang-si would say, "We can still use it." If it later broke, her reply came full circle: "No great loss; It was already cracked." So none of it was ever discarded but carefully wrapped and put aside for the mending man.

After inspecting everything that needed his attention and dickering for a price, he sat down on the back porch and went to work. Lining up the broken edges, he made little marks a quarter of an inch apart on opposite sides of the break. That done, he took out a tiny drill mounted on a six- to eight-inch metal post and looped it once with a piece of string attached at both ends to a wooden handle. The device resembled a loosely strung archery bow, though wider and shorter. Placing the drill point on the mark and holding the end of the post in his mouth, he carefully moved the bow back and forth to make a hole. Once in a while he'd stop to spit on his finger and wet the hole before continuing. Never once did he punch all the way through. Preparations complete, he took out metal "staples" to bridge the fracture that were exactly length of the space between the pairs of holes. If the surface was curved he used needle-nose tweezers to contour them to match. He carefully tested them, applied glue to the underside and to the broken edges, and firmly set them in place. The piece was whole once more and good as new until it met with further rough treatment.

One time Mother presented him with a real challenge. She had a lovely openwork milk-glass fruit bowl that was broken into a dozen pieces. It looked like a hopeless mess, but before the day was over he had restored it almost to its original glory.

We delighted in the visit of Mr. Hong, an artist. who came from a family in the south that practiced the ancient craft of burnt parchment drawing. Going from house to house, he displayed sample scrolls of typical Asian designs and offered to do something special and unique for each patron. Mother bought them for the "glory hole," her stash of gifts for others, and we brought him the best of our plain stationery to decorate.

"If you children want to watch, give Mr. Hong plenty of room. Don't get in his way, and stay away from his brazier," Mother warned.

"Here are some designs," he said. "Show me which ones you like."

"This one; it's the best," Jim said as he pointed to a dragon.

"No, it's too big," Betty protested. "How about the bamboo or the bent pine branch. . . or maybe that little cluster of birds. They're all nice".

"I'll have the baby chicks," Molly decided. "Aren't they cute?"

"Well, if the dragon is too big," Jim considered, "how about the rooster. I like the way his tail feathers arch up in back. I'm going to have roosters on my paper."

As we made our choices, the artist fanned the charcoal fire to red hot and thrust into it four miniature flatirons about the size of the end of your little finger. They were attached to slender, well-insulated, eight-inch rods. When all was ready Mr. Hong confirmed the designs we wanted, including a smaller version to go on the envelopes. He drew out an iron, blew away any clinging ash, tested it on a piece of wood, then went to work. His moves were so fast it was hard to see what he was doing as the images formed. A quick flick this way and that, and a flying bird appeared. Sometimes he used the pointed end to make a darker burn before easing up and turning the instrument on its side to make long, fast strokes, one after another. That's how he did the rooster's tail feathers. As soon as one iron cooled, he returned it to the fire and took out a hot one.

My bamboo appeared on the paper in lightning strokes. The stem was made with one long line accented twice with a slight hesitation. A little squiggle with the point of the iron indicated the joints. This way and that, the branches came next. Flick, flick, flick, and there were leaves. It left me breathless.

The job finished and the cost calculated, we were permitted to open our piggy banks (mine was a silver elephant) and count out the money we owed. That's how ordinary paper was turned into beautiful stationery, but nothing could equal the fascination of seeing him "paint" with his hot little irons.

I Beg to Differ with You, but. . .

Behold, how good and pleasant it is
to dwell together in unity!
Ps. 133:1

There were several rules in the family to which we paid close attention: mind your manners, speak the king's English, tell the truth, and never, ever, contradict Mother or Daddy.

"I wish I had a record that could be played all during mealtimes. It would save a lot of breath and give me more time to eat," Mother often said. She must have gotten heartily sick of continuous admonition. "Sit back and lean forward over your plate. Smaller bites, please. Keep your fingers out of your food—use a pusher (the exception was fried chicken). Chew your food longer; don't swallow it whole. Drink your milk more slowly. Wipe your mouth with your napkin, not with the back of your hand. Your elbows were not invited to the table." With eight of us to train, it went on for years, but the most effective instruction was what they modeled.

The same was true with our learning the king's English. No amount of studying rules of grammar could compare with hearing it spoken correctly every day. I am constantly amazed when I hear educated people in the pulpit, in the media, and in public speaking misuse sit and set, lie and lay, and I and me. For us no error went uncorrected.

"Who is it?" Mother asked when I'd knock on her bedroom door.

"It's me," I'd answer.

"Who is it?"

"It's me."

"*Who* is it?"

And finally I'd answer "Mother, *it is I.*"

The Wolfers, a refugee family from China, stayed with us for a few weeks before we left on furlough in 1925. They continued to occupy our house while we were gone until it was safe for them to return to their station. From the mid- to late 1920s many missionaries in China had to relocate on very short notice because of bandits. While in our house, a child was born to them. I guess ours was an exceptionally fine one for having babies.

Mrs. Wolfers told a tale that showed I wasn't the only one who got in trouble knocking on doors.

"I really had to get after our number one servant because he had the habit of knocking on our bedroom door, and opening it without being asked to come in. One day when he did it again I said to him, 'Al Ling, you must wait until I ask you to come in before you open the door. I might not be dressed, and we'd both be embarrassed.'"

Al Ling looked surprised. Then very well pleased with himself, he answered, "Never mind, Missie. Every time I look-see your keyhole. You no have clothes, I no come in."

Though carefully taught, we were not permitted to correct adults. When somebody from out of town said, "He don't." I was about correct to her, but I looked at Mother. Her lips were tightly pressed together, indicating that I should say nothing. Knowing what was good for me, I didn't.

Another imperative was telling the truth. There was no difference between a lie and a little white lie. They were all lies and were not tolerated. The punishment depended on circumstances, but it usually was a spanking.

One day Jimmy was very late for lunch. The rest of us were half-way through the meal when he arrived and was sent to wash his hands before sitting down.

"Didn't you hear the bell?" Daddy asked when he finally came to the table. "Why are you so late?"

"Well I saw Mrs. Ross down by her strawberry bed and had to tell her about my problem," he answered, looking very serious. "You see, I had this leg that was growing out from my side, and it made me walk crooked, so I went down to the hospital and the doctor cut it off." If ever there was a bald-faced lie, that was it, but Mother and Daddy seemed to be hiding laughter behind their napkins.

"Mother," I said, "you must spank Jimmy. He just told a big, big lie."

"I think your brother just has a very vivid imagination." She reached over and patted my hand.

From time to time he conjured up other strange tales, but we learned to accept them for what they were. Rolling our eyes, we'd simply say, "Yes, Jimmy has a very good imagination."

One thing not tolerated by either parent was talking back or being disrespectful. If we ever tried it, retribution was swift and sure. I didn't appreciated the discipline until one of my first years at Pyeng Yang Foreign School. Elizabeth (not her real name) and I were to share a room. Both of our mothers helped us settle in, hanging up clothes, arranging shoes, and making the beds. We were nearly finished when Elizabeth and her mother got into a strong disagreement on how her things were to be arranged. The woman never said a word and showed not the slightest concern when her daughter said all kinds of rude things to her. I was horrified, but mostly I felt sorry for Elizabeth and eternal gratitude to my parents for not allowing such behavior.

When we reached "the age of reason," if we wished to disagree with something that was said, we could do so politely by saying, "I beg to differ with you, but. . ." then we were permitted to speak our minds. We felt very grown up when we could enter freely into a discussion where strong opinions were expressed.

Away from home, I began to notice how adults got into heated arguments and sometimes were quite rude to each other. Mother and Daddy seemed to be in perfect agreement on everything. We thought it was the way all adults behaved. "Don't you and Daddy ever argue about anything? Do you agree all the time?" I asked Mother.

"Oh there are a lot of things we must work out, but we don't do it in front of you children. We either take a walk or wait until you are in bed and asleep." So that was it. They had arguments too, but they "worked them out" in private. But I do remember clearly two very strong disagreements they had, and they didn't try to hide them. We were teenagers, and I guess they thought we were old enough to understand.

The first one was on a point of scripture. Daddy read during family worship something to the effect that when we get to heaven we will all be the same before God. All our love will be toward Him and not toward those we know and love here on earth. Mother took strong exception to that bit of theology.

"Henry, you know very well that when we get to heaven I will love you more, a lot more than Tin-hoop-i," she said. Tin-hoop-i, the outside man, was not the smartest thing in long pants and was often the bane of her existence.

"No, Ruth, you won't. My understanding of the scripture is that the attachments we have here will be no more. We will focus our adoration on Jesus, and Jesus only ."

"I can't help it, dear. There is no way I'm going to love *that man* as much as I'll love you. I love you, and he nearly drives me crazy." I don't think the dispute was ever resolved.

The other argument had to do with Columbia, the cow.

When they decided to buy a milk cow they went to the market to see what was available. The animals were sold as beasts of burden only, never to provide milk. When a Korean baby was weaned at about the age of two, that was the end of its ration of milk.

Mother was a Nebraska girl and knew a few things about farm animals. Daddy, being a city kid, knew next to nothing, but they both knew that to have enough milk for all of us they needed a cow with a large udder. They found one that was half-Holstein and half-Ayrshire, providing both quantity and quality. After she was tested and found to be free of disease, they bought her.

There was no way to pasteurize milk, and Mother didn't like to boil it. She hired a couple to take care of the cow. The man was responsible for her feed (grown and prepared on the compound) and keeping the barn clean. Mother trained his wife to be an excellent milkmaid. The cow barn and their house were located just outside the mission compound. After washing her hands and the cow's udder and teats with soap and warm water, she squirted the milk right into a sterilized stainless steel pail covered with two sterile muslin cloths and a concave lid equipped with a fine mesh strainer. She immediately brought it the quarter-mile to our kitchen and poured it into glasses for the table and cooling pans for cooking.

Using the law of "supply and demand," Mother had Columbia milked three times a day instead of the usual two. She had it figured out just right. When the cow was fresh she gave twenty-one quarts a day. Every spring Columbia was allowed to go dry, and at the appropriate time a stud bull paid her a visit so we'd have a new calf in the fall and lots of milk.

"Our friend, Cho-si-bang, has a fine bull. He told me yesterday the cow should be serviced at the end of this month. I told him I'd let him know tomorrow about the time for him to come," Daddy said.

"Henry, the book says it is not time yet. If we want her to calve when we get back from the beach and not before, we should wait another six weeks. I really want to be here when she is due to make sure everything goes well." Mother was the one who took care of these matters. She did everything according to her book on the care and treatment of farm animals.

"Well, Ruth, this man really knows his business; he has done well by us in the past. If he says it's time, I think we should follow his suggestion."

"It's more likely that he wants his fee now, so he's asking for the earlier date. I don't like it. The book is right. I don't want Columbia to calve while we are away, so please tell Cho-si-bang he'll just have to wait."

Daddy wasn't too happy with Mother's faith in The Book. He was such an agreeable man; he'd probably told Cho-si-bang the earlier date was fine, and now he'd have to change it. Mother didn't always get her way, but nearly always!

Mixing It Up

A joyful heart is good medicine.
Prov. 17:22a

Jesus will wash away my sins, Jesus will wash away my sins (big sigh), Jesus will wash away my wubbers," three-year-old Willard sang to himself as he played with his teddy bear on the floor near Mother while she worked at her sewing machine.

As little children we learned Korean and English together and were truly bilingual, often interchanging words without understanding the difference. The Korean word *sin* means shoe, (pronounced *shin* in the South). A favorite hymn begins, "Oh happy day, oh happy day, when Jesus washed my sins away." Willard had it figured out that Jesus was going to wash away his *rubbers*.

We spoke Korean to the staff as they knew no English. To be polite to the occupying powers, we learned a few phrases in Japanese, such as "Good morning," "Good-bye," "Thank you," and "How much does it cost?" To each other we spoke English, and all our schooling was in English.

Living with two languages is fascinating. Many expressive Korean words were incorporated into our vocabulary. As a result, we spoke a grand mixture. A Korean word Mother used often was *pup,* meaning recipe. There was no such thing as being able to follow directions right from an American cookbook. Substitutions were made for items not available in the Korean market. Pups that worked on a wood-burning stove and with limited ingredients were a constant subject of conversation among the women.

Beef was tough. Cows were beasts of burden and slaughtered when ready to die of old age; thus roasts and steaks never graced our table. Instead we had stews, pot roasts, and ground meat, very lean.

On a special occasion when a board member from the States came to visit, we held a station dinner at our house.

"Is it true that Koreans eat dogs?" the guest asked.

"Yes," Mother answered, "and it seems that black dogs are favored over brown or white."

At the pot-luck dinner Mother provided a meat loaf made from a new recipe she found in a magazine just out from the States. One of the neighbors, savoring a bite asked her, "Ruth, is this the new *pup*?"

"Yes," she answered, "and I think it turned out quite well, don't you?" The guest didn't eat any meat that night!

Many Korean words sounded alike to us, and often we made funny mistakes much to their delight. A room in our basement had half the floor in soft earth for burying root vegetables to keep them fresh and safe from freezing during the winter. The words for celery, *may*-na-*di*, and daughter-in-law, may-*ne-ry*, are similar. Once Mother said to the outside man, "Today, please dig up the may-*ne-ry* and bury her in the basement." Another time she handed a coat with a missing a button to the sewing woman, asking her to please sew a jackass on it.

Dr. Ross, senior missionary in our Syenchun Station, was embarrassed one very hot Sunday when a member of the congregation approached him after the service.

"*Moksa-nim* (honorable pastor), I'll try to follow your teaching, but how can we help sweating on a day like this?" The words for "covet" and "sweat" are almost the same. Dr. Ross had preached a long, learned sermon on "Thou Shalt Not Sweat!"

We had many a good laugh over some mistakes the Koreans made, too, as they struggled to learn English. Daddy met Mr. Kim downtown the day after he and his wife had dinner at our house.

"Oh, Dr. Lampe," he said in his best English, "we enjoy dinner at your house so much. I tank you from the bottom of my heart, and my wife tanks you from her bottom too."

One of the missionaries in Pyeng Yang was known for her very careful language, so everybody was much amused when they heard about her spoonerism. One Saturday morning, her son Dayton was playing with Sam Moffett. She went to the door and called, "Sam and Dayton, come for lunch." They didn't come, so once again she called. Getting exasperated when they still didn't show, she raised her voice and called again, "Dam and Satan, come in for lunch this minute!"

God Has No Grandchildren

And Jesus said unto him,
"I am the way, the truth, and the life;
no one comes to the Father, but through me."
John 14:6

As far back as I can remember I knew God loved me. To think of Him being nearby, always caring, always ready to help, was as natural as breathing. The focus of our family life was living in harmony with each other in obedience to God. I wouldn't have stated it just that way, but in retrospect I can see that it was so.

As sheltered as our home life was, we saw clear evidence that not everybody shared our faith. The large majority of Koreans practiced Animism, and spirit worship was central to their lives. If somebody became ill, an evil spirit was to blame and had to be driven away.

Infants cry, especially when teething. It hurts. If the crying persisted, tradition convinced the parents an evil spirit was responsible. It was provided a way out by placing a red hot coin on the child's scalp. Apparently boys had lots of problems as evidenced by the small bald spots on their heads which showed up when their hair was cut short for school. If nothing else, the burning was a counterirritant, but it left a permanent mark.

A popular way to banish evil spirits was by having a *moo-dong,* hiring a shaman to perform the rites. In a long, colorful robe and ornate headdress, she danced to the beat of drums and clashing cymbals. The din could be heard a mile away, and the ceremony lasted for hours. I have no idea how much success they claimed.

Bill Chisholm was our doctor in Syenchun. He was of medium height, almost completely bald, and had bright blue eyes and a ready smile. He exuded strength, and his hands were skilled and strong. He, like most mission doctors, was a general practitioner who faced every kind of challenge. They performed surgery, delivered babies, diagnosed illnesses, and treated them to the best of their ability. Before the days of sulfa drugs and antibiotics, prayer and aspirin went a long way.

Dr. Chisholm frequently told of trying to save people after they had suffered at the hands of the local witch doctor. Once he removed ten pounds of chipped plowshare from a farmer's stomach. The sorcerer had prescribed it to cure a bad stomach ache. On another occasion he removed twelve long needles from a man's abdomen that had been inserted to let the devil out .

Even higher education didn't seem to give them hope that there might be a better way. A wealthy member of the Oh family had been to college in America. He was known as "Brickhouse Oh" because he had a very grand red-brick house on the edge of town. He was not a Christian but used the hospital when his family needed medical attention.

One night after the Chisholms had gone to bed, there was a loud pounding on the front door. A messenger, out of breath after peddling his bike up the steep hill, gasped out, "*Weesa-Nim* (honorable doctor), please come quickly. The Ohs' infant son is desperately ill. No one but you can save him. You must come at once." After ten years of marriage the baby was their only child, and he was dying. Unfortunately, the Christian hospital was chosen as a last resort. A *moo-dong* had failed, and the baby's condition worsened. Minutes before he entered the baby's hospital room, they had split open a live chicken and placed it on his chest. Amid the blood and feathers he got an IV going; but the pneumonia was too far advanced, and the baby died that night.

We felt so blessed comparing our care to that of the poor kids whose heads were burned and people who had needles stuck into their stomachs and all sorts of other terrible things done to them. We wished they could feel as safe and happy as we did. Many of their problems stemmed from their belief in spirits. Daddy claimed he could tell who were Christians and who were not. There is such fear connected with Animism that it showed on their faces. If they knew Jesus as we did, how much better for them!

Animists are careful to give the devil his due. In each home a wicker basket hangs close to the ceiling near a wall. A part of everything coming into the house belongs to the spirit—be it a handful of rice or a few inches of cloth cut from the end of a length of material. Whatever is put into the basket belongs to the spirit and cannot be removed, even dust. As soon as one basket is full another is hung next to it.

When an Animist becomes a Christian, one of the first things he wants to do is get rid of the baskets, yet the very idea of going against such a long-held belief is hard. After singing and praying, a pastor and several elders cleansed the house. Daddy witnessed several such events. The new Christian didn't dare go near it. Shaking, and turning white with fear, he stood in the road at least fifty yards away to watch until every basket was burned and all traces of Animism had been removed and thrown into the fire.

In the later years of his ministry, Daddy drove his car between the major North Korean cities, but it was no joy ride. There were no paved roads. The "highway" was a rutted bull-cart path, regularly spread with rocks, which over time were broken down and pressed into a hard surface by a stream of carts, cars, and jitneys. It was slow going. Punctures and blowouts were a regular and anticipated part of travel. Three in a day's trip were not unusual, but there was a still greater hazard to face.

"I get more gray hairs from driving than from anything else," he'd complain. "As I get up a good, breakneck speed of twenty-five miles an hour, some woman walking on the roadside, usually with a big load on her head, dashes across the road just in front of me. Jamming on the brakes and swerving in the opposite direction are the only ways to avoid hitting her. It's enough to give me a heart attack, but so far I've only grazed a few."

It was all tied to the belief that a one-eyed, one-legged *tok-kabbie,* a demon mischief-maker, hops along behind a person and is responsible for all his trouble. The idea of running in front of a fast-moving car was to make the encounter just close enough to escape injury but to squash the hated *tok-kabbie.*

There was no danger that we children would be attracted to the strange beliefs that surrounded us. We were carefully taught the tenets of the Christian faith through daily family worship, memorizing scripture, and the example of our parents. There was no doubt in my mind that my best friend was Jesus, and I wanted it to be that way always. Along with the blessings we enjoyed came responsibilities. Mother and Daddy pointed out that their faith was not sufficient for our salvation. I can still hear them saying, "God has no grandchildren. To be a Christian each person must make his own commitment to God." Well, there it was in the back of my head, but I didn't feel any urgency in doing anything about it.

My high school rogues' gallery picture

Mother's Stories

We spend our years as a tale that is told.
Ps. 90:9

In our missionary home in the North Korea of the 1920s and 1930s, the only mechanical form of entertainment we had was a wind-up Victrola. Our record library consisted of two or three dozen platters by Stephen Foster, Harry Lauder, and Ethelbert Nevin. Life was rich, however, with games, reading, and storytelling. The hour before bedtime was a high point of the day. We took turns choosing our favorites from Mother's collection of children's books. She also entertained us with tales of her childhood that we delighted to hear over and over again.

Our lifestyle was as close to that in the States as Mother and Daddy could make it. We were home-schooled but lived cross-culturally with the Koreans. We returned to the States for a year's furlough after seven in Korea. We were rooted there, it was home, but we yearned for a closer connection to our parents' heritage. Mother's stories helped us feel we, too, belonged to our native land through her experiences.

She was born in Ponca, Nebraska, a small farming community in the northeastern part of the state. Her father, Nathan Heydon, and mother, Irene, were pioneers in the Nebraska Territory.

"When I was a little girl, we didn't have running water. Each family had a well a few yards from the house. We kept several animals, a cow for milk, two horses to pull the buggy and cart, chickens, a dog, and a cat.

"One day Father was puzzled. He just couldn't figure out why the horses wouldn't drink. He checked them over, and they seemed to be fine. Mother, my sister Helen, and I were startled the next day when Dad came storming into the house, slammed the door, and noisily emptied every water container in the kitchen.

"Nathan, what in the world is the matter?" Mother asked him.

"'I was checking up on the animals and found out what's wrong," he raged. "Remember last week when that band of gypsies came through and asked to camp on our property and I let them? Well, they thanked us by throwing a dead baby into the well, and that's why the horses haven't been drinking," he shouted, stamping his foot in disgust. "I'll get some help to remove the baby and see to its burial. Then I'll find out what's needed to clean the water. In the meantime, Ruth, you and Helen take pails to the Hanson's, wash them out carefully, and bring home water to clean everything in the kitchen. Go back and get more for us to drink. It will be some time before we can use our well again. Gypsies!' he roared. 'Just wait 'til they come again next year!"

Mother as a young girl

We all made faces, thinking how awful it would be to drink water that had a dead baby floating in it; then we waited for Mother's next story.

"On a warm June day when I was one of the older girls permitted to sit at the back of our one-room school, I was busy studying when the teacher spoke sharply to me.

'Ruth Heydon,' she said. 'come here to my desk at once.' "I was startled because I had been working hard. I hadn't been whispering or passing notes or anything. I really didn't know what was the matter, and it frightened me. I got up and went to her. She had a stern look on her face, but it wasn't an angry one. When I got there she stood up. I felt so ashamed because all the others in the room were looking at me.

"I didn't mean to upset you, but I did want you to move quickly,' she said.

"She took my hands in hers and turned me around. There on the wall shelf above the coat hooks, right behind my chair, was a big black snake!"

That was our signal to squeal and pull our feet in close, looking to make sure there were no big black snakes in our house!

"Now off to bed," Mother announced. "Call when you're ready to say your prayers, and don't forget to brush your teeth."

What exciting times our mother lived in, I thought, with horses and buggies to ride in, and even Indians not far away. But things were not so different in Korea. Under Japanese rule we were safe, yet just fifty miles north on the Manchurian border, bandit raids were common, and people were killed or carried off for ransom.

Mother as a teenager

Christmas in Syenchun

. . . know how to give good gifts unto your children.
Matt. 7:11

The moment Heydon, Willard, Cordelia, and Nathan returned home from boarding school, we made a ceremonial trip up the hill to cut down a Christmas tree and drag it home.

"Come on, you little squirts," Willard said, "let's go find the prettiest tree up there. You can hold it steady while Heydon and I chop it down." The first half of the family was enough older than the rest of us that we considered them to be full of wisdom and a lot of fun with all kinds of new ideas. We gladly did their bidding, whatever it was they asked. When the task was completed, Mother rewarded us with cups of steaming-hot cocoa. Wrapping our hands around the mugs helped to warm icy fingers. Trouble was, I always seemed to burn my tongue.

The tree was set up in the living room right in front of the windows. We decorated it with paper chains, popcorn strings, ornaments made of colored paper, and little candles in tin holders that we clamped onto the branches carefully to make sure they wouldn't catch fire. While on furlough in the States in 1934, we bought some beautiful glass balls, icicles, and silver rain that added a lively sparkle.

We lovingly wrapped our gifts in paper we decorated ourselves. Using a comb, colored water, and a brush, we made splatterwork designs with pressed leaves and cutouts. Mother gave us helpful hints as to what she would like to receive such as little booklets made of pieces of fabric that she could use as pen wipers, great for the days of leaky fountain pens.

There being no candy on the market except for *yut* (a Korean taffy), Mother set aside several evenings to concoct special treats for the season. Peanut brittle was the most fun to make because it was so easy, but fondant was another story. Mother cooked up a big pot of it that had to ripen until it was just right for making into individual candies. After dinner when the dishes had been cleared away, she spread an oilcloth covering on the table, and we were each given a handful to work. We'd press it, squeeze it, and if a few crumbs fell, we could taste it—I noticed that Jimmy's was unusually crumbly. As soon as it was smooth and creamy, we'd add color and flavoring. Pink was for peppermint, green for wintergreen, yellow for black walnut, and white for vanilla. We fashioned it into all sorts of shapes—balls, cubes, thin rectangles with nuts pressed in, or whatever else pleased us. The fondant thus flavored, colored, and shaped was allowed to rest in the cold pantry for twenty-four hours before dipping.

We could only get bitter baking chocolate, but we didn't know anything else, so that was fine. Chocolate was hard to come by, and to make it go farther a little paraffin was added. It also made the candy look nice and shiny. Then came the dipping, each flavor being segregated so a selection could be made without mistake. Biting into it was wonderful. The bitter-sweet contrast was the best of all.

Each year we filled bags with cookies, candy, and fruit for the postman and others who came to the door during the holiday season. The servants made garlands of pine to twine around the banister and hang over every door. A sprig decorated each picture. The house took on a festive look and smelled wonderful from the mixture of baking cookies and pies, pine, and polished wood. Gift wrapping, whispered secrets, having everyone home added up to unbearable excitement.

Best of all, Christmas day was Mother's birthday. Since the station dinner that night would be her birthday party, at breakfast we had a special bit of celebration including an angelfood cake, which was 100 percent better than oatmeal. We tried to hide the cake, but she invariably found it "by accident," one year in the laundry hamper. We could always count on Daddy taking an inordinate amount of time with *kito*. Before breakfast we received our stockings that had been hung from the mantel Christmas Eve during the singing of "Jolly Old St. Nicholas," but the tree had to wait until after family worship, and Daddy made a big thing of it. It seemed we would never get to the tree.

At last, one by one we opened the most wonderful gifts. It was a rapturous surprise when Betty and I received dolls that Mother had made. She had stuffed the bodies and attached composition heads, arms, and feet ordered from Montgomery Ward. Their eyes didn't open and close, but they were soft and huggable and our very own. She had also made them lots of clothes. That same Christmas I received storybooks to read after supper and a special party dress Mother had made with beautiful smocking on the front and around the puffed sleeves. Santa brought me a little purse all the way from America.

A wall in the dining room was designated the Rogue's Gallery. Hunkey carved an appropriate sign, and as we went away to school, Mother made sure she had pictures to hang there. They were placed in order according to age with Heydon, Willard, Hunkey, and Nathan in the first row; Betty, I, Jim, and Molly in the second. As we married, the arrangement shifted around to accommodate additions. The Christmas gift Mother requested of the ones going away to college was a new picture.

Hunkey started her freshman year while we were on furlough. The next Christmas, Mother naturally wanted a picture of her for the gallery, but packages from the States took forever. Each time the postman arrived, she looked for an appropriate box, but there was none.

Daddy, Mother and the Rogues' gallery.

"Oh, well, there's still time. Perhaps it will come tomorrow," she'd say in disappointment. As the days moved toward December 25, there was still nothing. Christmas Eve came and went. I knew she was terribly upset and sometimes looked ready to cry.

I could hardly contain myself because I had Hunkey's picture! Count on her to pull a fast one. She had mailed it to the Underwoods before they left the States in the fall, and they brought it in their luggage as far as Seoul. I picked it up on my bimonthly orthodontic trip to the city just before Christmas vacation. I packed it at the bottom of my suitcase. It was such an important secret that all four of us managed to keep it, though we saw the pain Mother was suffering as she looked in vain for its arrival.

On Christmas Eve when everybody was in bed, I crept downstairs and put it, unwrapped, under the tree, covering it with other gifts. We were all present when Mother came out and glanced around. Nothing. While we had our stockings and ate breakfast, she tried bravely to look cheerful. Betty pinched me under the table, and I poked Jim when he got a silly grin on his face.

Daddy knew about the picture. He had a way of moving his shoulders when he was tickled about something, and that morning they seemed to be in constant motion. After worship he finally started handing out the gifts. From the tree's branches he took a few small ones that we opened with gusto, but Mother looked sad. When he could stand it no longer, he stooped down, pulled out Hunkey's picture, and took to her. Her surprised face radiated joy as she reached out with both hands to receive it, held it to her chest, and broke into tears.

All day long she kept looking at it, caressing the frame, and tracing Hunkey's features with her finger. She had her cry and looked up at me.

"You little scamp! How in the world did you manage without my knowing?"

"It wasn't easy," I said with a laugh, "but you know Hunkey. If something can be done in an unusual way, she'll do it."

For some reason Christmas lunch was always cornmeal mush. Mother must have figured it was all our stomachs could take on such an exciting day, and there was an enormous dinner to look forward to that night. Christmas was unbelievably marvelous, and when it was over the next one always seemed light years away.

Sorai Beach

Thou has made summer and winter.
Ps. 74:17

Rivaling the anticipation of Christmas was getting ready for our summer trip to Sorai (pronounced *sorry*) Beach. It began at midnight when we boarded the train in Syenchun. We younger children went to bed early and tried to get some rest because there would be little sleep in our lumpy third-class bunks. All kinds of goodies were neatly packed in boxes for our meals on the way.

The older kids made the trip by car with Daddy two days ahead of us. When our train arrived at the station nearest Sorai Beach midmorning of the second day, they were there. With all of us crammed into the car and the baggage strapped on the running board, top, and back, we headed off for the last twenty-five miles to the ocean.

Excitement built as we passed familiar places along the road where we had stopped for a picnic, a flat tire, or somebody needing to find some bushes. As we emerged from the mountain pass and saw the glittering waters of the Yellow Sea, we went wild. We inhaled deep breaths of fragrant salt air and could think only of our first swim.

The moment we had the doors of the house open and the shutters up, Mother handed out the bathing suits she had wisely packed right at the top of a suitcase. No amount of hunger, thirst, or weariness slowed us down. In five minutes all who could swim dashed down the hill on Bright Angels Trail for a first dip. It was nothing short of heaven on earth.

Life at the beach was relaxed and informal. Syenchun was a small station of just a few families and three single women, so it was a tremendous boon for Mother and Daddy to enjoy friends from other cities and devour books for which there was no time during the long winter. We kids had a chance to meet all kinds of wonderful people our own ages.

We had a choice of three summer resorts. Chiri San was in the mountains at an elevation of eight thousand feet, and Wan San was a beach on the east coast; but we knew Sorai Beach was far superior to the others.

Each cottage had a name, and the Lampes' was naturally called The Beacon. Painted light yellow with a green tin roof, it was easily identified from the highway across the bay.

The inside walls were unvarnished pine. One of the supporting beams became a measuring post for recording our heights at the beginning of each summer. The wall separating the dining room from the kitchen was our "guest book." Anyone sharing a meal with us was invited to sign it. Over the years several who had been our guests died. Daddy carefully varnished over their names to preserve them for all time.

The dining room took up half of the front of the house on the ground floor, and two of the boys used the opposite side as a bedroom. The open floor plan meant they had to keep everything neatly picked up. At the rear was the kitchen, cook's room, and garage. When the three oldest came home from college the garage was made into a bedroom so the whole family could fit—all ten of us!

The second-floor walls were only eight feet high, leaving an open space up to the pointed roof that allowed the movement of cool air. The stairs were in the middle of the house; the living room occupied the front half, and the back contained two bedrooms, each with a pair of single beds. At both ends of the living room long, tin-lined boxes held bedding, linens, and clothing because Mother and Daddy slept on the daybed. Topped with comfortable pads, the boxes provided extra seating. We called the larger one Daddy's coffin and the smaller one Mother's. Such irreverent terminology took people by surprise.

It's a wonder we ended up with straight, strong backs, considering what we slept on. Bed frames were made of two-by-fours with rope laced from side to side and head to toe, and the mattresses were large sacks filled with dry seaweed. When we were small and had "accidents," no problem. The seaweed was discarded, the sack washed and refilled. Sometimes lumps prevented a comfortable rest, so we worked them out by pulling them apart and evening the mass. Trying to get comfortable reminded me of the way our dog went round and round in her basket before lying down.

A seventy-five-foot-high peninsula jutted into the sea, curving on its leeward side, thus protecting a pure-white, sandy beach from heavy winds and surf. It was ideal for swimming. Tides ran very high, but the beach sloped so gently that one could walk out quite a distance and still be only waist deep. Three tripods anchored at hundred-yard intervals contributed to safety and fun for the swimmers, and about 150 yards beyond the last tripod floated a raft with a low diving board. During the principal swimming hours morning and afternoon, men took turns serving as lifeguards in a rowboat, staying near any swimmers who looked unsure of themselves. Because of the fine combination of nature and human effort, there wasn't a single drowning in all of its history.

On both sides of the bluff, above the beach, and all along the windward side perched the summer cottages of association members. I thought ours very grand, overlooking the ocean, lowlands, and mountains in the distance. It cost all of two-hundred dollars to build in 1925. Originally we had a little bungalow, but when the family grew it was torn down and replaced. "If I had charged admission to see how we all got to bed in that tiny house, we would have had enough money to build the new one," Mother said.

Sorai Beach's enviable safety record was due in part to the childrens' swimming-achievements program. Accomplishing the first step entitled the participant to sew a large white S on his swimsuit. At the age of five I was the youngest ever to win the award. The circle, which was more difficult, fit around the S. I didn't earn it until a couple of years after I got my wings at the age of six. To earn them you had to swim the point. The Ludlow Cup competition was held at the end of the summer, and the point swim counted for half of the total score. The course was a mile and a quarter, starting at the float, going around the point, along the bluff, ending at the fishing village at the far end of the Association's property. Men in boats anchored every two-hundred yards made sure no swimmer was without help if he got a cramp or just wanted to give it up. The time of the race was carefully planned to make use of the tide. Fifteen minutes before it finished running out the race began, giving contestants plenty of time to round the end of the point, where the strong incoming tide carried them down the bay.

Older swimmers made quick work of it, but for the younger ones it was a long haul. I was a pretty good dog-paddler I guess, because an hour and a half after I jumped off the float, I was hauled aboard the *Black Duck* at the finish line and wrapped in a blanket. As friendly hands wiped the grime off my face, happy words of congratulations filled my ears. Someone handed me a big mug of hot cocoa, just the thing for one so cold and tired, and it got the salty taste out of my mouth.

"Ruth, which of your children are swimming today?" one of Mother's friends asked,

"We're watching Frances," she said as she, Betty, and Jim followed my progress on the bluff. "If she finishes, she'll be the youngest ever to swim the point, and we're here to cheer her on."

"You mean to tell me you've permitted that little bit of a girl make such a long swim? Ruth, I'm really surprised!"

"Well," she answered, "there are the boats to help her if she needs it, but it's my guess she'll finish. She's our little fish!" Most of the crowd had gone ahead to greet the swimmers as they came in, but my rooting section stayed with me, waving a big white dishtowel as they saw me look up at them.

After a short rest on the *Black Duck* I swam to shore, where Daddy, wearing tennis shoes to protect his feet against the slippery, barnacle-covered rocks, was waiting for me in water up to his waist. Spectators who had followed the race from the bluff gathered at the beach to cheer the swimmers finishing the course. A big one went up when Daddy emerged with me on his back. Overcome by shyness, I scrunched down, but he made me straighten up and thank them. I knew he was proud of me.

We had family tradition that any one who swam the point could have a cup of coffee. (After sixteen, one was offered on Sunday mornings.) I relished my very first taste with lots of sugar and cream. Jim wasn't so lucky the day he became eligible. He loved the smell of coffee and could hardly wait to try it. We marched triumphantly back to the house, and while we rinsed off with buckets of fresh water (we had nothing so grand as a shower or bathtub) and dressed, Mother brewed a pot. Most ceremoniously, she poured a cup for Jim. He took a sip and made a terrible face. He just couldn't believe it! Why didn't it taste as good as it smelled? In spite of such a letdown, the honor of having made the swim carried the day. I was proud of my little brother.

One morning when I was fourteen I woke up feeling terrible. My head ached, and I could tell I was running a fever because my eyes felt hot. I went down to breakfast, but after one look at me, Mother sent me back to bed.

"As soon as we finish *kito*," she said, "I'll see what we can do for you." I could hardly wait to get into my lovely, lumpy bed.

Two days before, Molly had rescued a little kitten that was being tormented by some Korean boys. They were trying to hang it, and hearing its choking cries, she got it away from them.

"Can I keep the kitty?" she asked Mother.

"You mean 'may I,' don't you?"

"May I please, please, please?"

"Yes, you may, but first let's clean it up."

We carefully groomed the little thing but evidently missed some fleas. As I lay on the bed reading that afternoon, the kitten curled up in the crook of my knee. The next day a small blister appeared on my leg, surrounded by a large red, very sore area.

Dr. Smith from next door came over to see me. He decided to give me aspirin and see what developed. In a short time we had the answer—Manchurian or relapsing fever. A day later Molly got it too. The fever wasn't high, but our neck glands were swollen, and dark yellow jaundice followed. What misery! No appetite, a terrible headache, and I didn't even want to go swimming, an unthinkable state at Sorai Beach. Mother moved our beds into the living room where we would be cooler during the heat of the day.

"Hey, you look terrible. Even your eyes are yellow!" I said after one look at Molly.

"Have you seen yourself in the mirror?" She groaned.

For a week we lived on thin soup and dry bread. As the jaundice faded our skin flaked away, leaving us with a mighty itch all over. By the end of the week and just as we were beginning feel human again, the fever flared briefly before disappearing altogether. We were two wobbly kids as we went for our first swim, and was it good—almost like being reborn.

We lived next door to the Underwoods. Dr. Underwood was the son of the first Presbyterian missionary in Korea and was president of Chosun Christian College, now Yonsei University. He was of stocky build and rather short compared to Daddy and my brothers, but I always sensed that he was very strong, both physically and mentally. He had bushy eyebrows and piercing blue eyes. He smoked too, which was considered scandalous, but folks simply didn't talk about it. He smoked, and that was the end of it.

Mrs. Underwood came to Korea with the Methodist Mission to establish a school for missionary children. After a few years of courting, they were married and had five children. Horace was Hunkey's age; the twins, James and John were Betty's age; Dick was Jim's, and Grace a year or two younger than Molly.

Mrs. Underwood was very short and well rounded but not fat. Like Mother she combed her hair back from her face into a bun. The most remarkable thing about her was her broad and generous smile. When she was thinking of something she wanted to say in exactly the right way, she had a habit of pursing her lips, and you knew you were in for some special wisdom or a good joke. She was definitely a no-nonsense person; we obeyed quickly when she spoke, and she was always fair.

I often thought that if I didn't have Mother and Daddy, I'd want to be in the Underwood family. They had a wonderful way of listening attentively. They didn't talk down to me as if I was a little kid, which I was. Dr. Underwood encouraged me in my swimming, and Mrs. Underwood urged me on as I undertook other projects. One summer a silver cup was offered to the person who could collect, identify, press, mount, and display the greatest number of local wild flowers. I won it, mostly because of her enthusiasm. The following summer brought a contest for shells, and I won that too. I just felt good around the Underwoods.

They were related to the Underwood Typewriter family and benefited from an inheritance that made it possible for them to enjoy some extras that they generously shared. We had no money for anything beyond what was absolutely necessary, but we weren't poor. "Poverty is a state of mind, not the size of your bank account," was Daddy's philosophy.

The Underwoods' twenty-five-foot *Black Duck.* comfortably accommodated ten to twelve people, and they often took others to the islands for picnics and overnight outings. Everybody was invited at least once during the summer. They passed our house on the way to the beach, so if somebody couldn't go at the last moment one or two of the lucky Lampes were asked to fill in. Oh joy!

On one such day when Nathan was home for the summer, he was invited. Pushing off from shore, Dr. Underwood tried to start the engine. The Johnson Seahorse was the best to be had in the late 1930s, yet it was anything but reliable. The starter cord wasn't permanently attached. You had to set a knot at the end of the rope into a slot, wind it up, and give it a hard yank. For a half hour the boat went around and around and around in circles as the men tried to get it going. It merely sputtered a few times and died.

"Mrs. Underwood watched until she could stand it no longer," Nathan said, telling of his adventure. "She got up and told us all to get out of the way. 'I'll show you how to do it,' she boasted. She followed the procedure, braced her foot, and hollered, 'Now, damn it, start!' The engine roared to life. She looked at me and winked. 'You see, that's all it needed!'"

With good swimmers in both families, we decided one summer that we'd try to capture and hold all the beatable records. I set out to take the record for girls doing the race to Mysterious Island.

After several weeks of training by running three miles on the sand every morning before breakfast, I was ready. Without fanfare, Daddy and I borrowed a rowboat and went. The tide was right, and it was calm most of the way. He kept a little ahead of me so I could sense where he was.

It was my first experience with getting a second wind. Just when the agony of continuing seemed too great to take another stroke, it happened. All of a sudden the pain and breathlessness were gone, and I could take long, even strokes. I felt as if I were inside a body that was carrying me along without any effort on my part. Several times the pain came back, but by staying with it, I got a third and a fourth wind. I touched shore in two hours and fifty-four minutes—an hour longer than the record held by James and John Underwood, but shaving minutes off the previous one held by women.

I was the first at Sorai Beach with a halter top!

Clam Island

. . . and when I saw . . . I wondered with great admiration.
Rev. 17:6

Mysterious and Starfish were the nearest of the islands that formed a ring around our bay. They lay four and a half miles to the west, just off the mainland near the gap where the highway came through the mountains and followed the coast to Sorai Beach. Clam Island was at the other end of the bay, appearing to be just off the tip of the mainland, although it was twelve miles away. In between were Big Blue, Little Blue, and White Wing, twenty-five miles out.

James and John, the Underwood twins, were inseparable. The previous winter James had nearly died of spinal meningitis and was still weak from the ordeal. John wanted to try the swim to Clam Island even though James couldn't. It was their last summer at Sorai Beach before leaving for college in the States and a final chance to make the long swim.

The first time John tried it strong currents swept him past his goal, so before making another attempt, he and his father planned carefully, estimating his speed and checking the tide. He started before dawn, wearing a woolen tank suit and having most of his body covered with heavy car grease to keep him warm. Dr. Underwood went with him in one of the small boats, the *Duckling*; the rest of us followed after breakfast in the *Black Duck*.

Willard, Hunkey, and I were among several who paced John, swimming a few yards ahead so he could save his energy by sensing our presence without having to look up. We took half-hour turns, but John was such a strong swimmer it was hard to keep ahead of him even though we were fresh. Willard was with him when he made the last sprint to the beach, and even he, one of the best, couldn't keep up.

Before starting out John had said to his father he thought he could make it in six hours and forty minutes. When he touched land the stopwatch showed exactly six hours and forty-two minutes. For several years I had a crush on John, so I felt most honored to have a part in his great achievement. On our way home he rested in the cabin, all bundled up in blankets.

"Is there anything I can do for you?" I poked my head in and asked.

"Sure, give me a kiss," he said. I didn't oblige. I mean, you just didn't go around kissing boys even if you did like them a lot; but it did give my heart an extra flip to know that the idea had crossed his mind.

Ten years later my husband, Kedar, our three children, and I stayed with the Underwoods in Seoul for six weeks while a house was being made ready for us. At dinner the night of our arrival John was late, held up at a meeting. He came in while we were eating and was introduced to Kedar. He said hello to me and sat down.

"Well, I'm disappointed," Kedar said after a moment or two of silence. Everybody looked startled.

"Why, what's the matter?"

"I expected John to come in and sweep Fran off her feet," Kedar answered. "She's been telling me for years that John was her secret passion when she was a girl. All he does when he sees her is to say hello."

Three Lost Maidens

He delivereth and rescueth.
Dan. 6:27

All was quiet because twelve boatloads from the Beach were on a week's cruise to the outer islands. Hunkey, Fan Campbell, a girl my age, and I decided to borrow one of the Underwood's Old Town canoes, paddle to Starfish Island, cook our supper, and return before dark. The water was calm, and with our parents' blessing we left around two in the afternoon.

It was an easy trip over. Starfish is very small and uninhabited, so we anticipated picnicking without drawing a crowd. Along the shoreline lay a large bank of bright fan shells of all colors and in perfect condition. Every trip we selected a few to take home. The water was crystal clear as we swam around huge pillars of weathered rock coming right up from the sea. Gentle waves nudged us against them as we floated, watching fish dart in and out, nibbling on sea weed and crustaceans. As the sun lost its sting and the air cooled, we built a fire, cooked our supper, and after eating, sat talking.

The Underwoods had a tradition of keeping a lantern atop their flagpole at night when boats were away from the beach. If any should return in the dark, they could see the light and plot their course. Because of it, we weren't afraid of returning after sunset.

Sitting right under a high bluff, we were completely unaware that a furious summer storm was approaching. We launched the canoe and started toward home when all of a sudden it engulfed us. In no time, winds whipped up huge waves, lifting the spray and dashing it in our faces. Crackling lightning and ear-splitting thunder surrounded us. The sky was black. Mysterious Island was only two hundred yards away, and at low tide its far end was connected to the mainland by a sand bar.

"Let's try for it," Hunkey screamed into the wind. We paddled furiously, but it was useless. Our bodies acted as sails, and we were going backwards.

She and I jumped overboard, Fan got as low as she could in the middle, and we swam the canoe back to the cove. With the wind pushing us the return was quick, and as soon as we rounded the sheltering cliff the water was quiet.

The Old Town canoe was heavy. It took two strong men to carry it down to the water from the boathouse, but we were so scared that as soon as Fan stepped onto the beach, Hunkey and I each took an end and ran up the steep shell bank.

The storm last only a half hour, but the sky didn't clear enough for us to see the Underwood light. Not remembering the tide schedule, we thought it prudent to stay put until dawn. It was a chilly, dark night. Our only shelter was a cave full of bats, so we huddled together on a rock ledge, sharing the damp towels in an effort to ward off hungry mosquitoes. The tops of Hunkey's legs were warm with sunburn, so Fan hugged one and I the other.

Well after midnight we heard voices. We kept quiet; if they were casual fishermen we didn't want to invite their attention. When they came near, we could hear them singing as they rowed just off shore. In Korean native tradition they made up verses to suit the occasion.

"Three young maidens went out in a boat, tra-la-la-la-la-la,
And they have been lost at sea, tra-la-la-la-la-la.
Their parents are worried about their safety, tra-la-la-la-la-la,
And have hired us to go out to the rescue, tra-la-la-la-la-la."

We were relieved to know they were looking for us. Hearing our call, two fishermen came to the beach, helped us into their little boat, and gave us a thermos of hot coffee and some blankets. Canoe in tow, they rowed with a fishtail oar to the far end of Mysterious Island, where Daddy stood on the beach in the early morning light. As we approached, I wondered if this is how Jesus looked to the desciples after they'd been out all night.

A dress Mother made of real fishnet; fanshell buttons from Starfish Island

The Dark Side

There is an appointed time for everything.
And there is a time for every event under heaven—
A time to embrace, and a time to shun embracing.
Eccl. 3: 1, 5b

The summer I was fifteen I began to look less like a boy as I filled out in the appropriate places.

Our family was invited to the Monroe's* for lunch, after which Mother asked me to help clean up and take back to our house the uneaten food we'd brought. It was time for everybody to meet on the beach for the 4th of July celebration.

Mr. Monroe was the only one there when I dashed into the living room to see if there was anything left. He held out his arms for a big hug. He was a very affectionate man, and we all thought of him as a nice big teddy bear. This time it was different. He pulled me, pressing himself hard against me. In a moment it was over; I broke free and fled. I was baffled and never told anyone.

That same year quite a few mishkids were home from college for the summer, bringing extra enjoyment to the life of the community. Heydon, Willard, and Nathan were among them. Cordelia had spent the year in Korea, so our whole family was together for the first time in ages. It was wonderful. Mother and Daddy were in their glory.

We younger ones loved to be around our sophisticated elders. They seemed to be so far above us and full of the stories of their adventures in the States. We hung on every word. It was exciting to think that in a few years we too would be venturing out into that wonderful world.

One day a group of them was playing water polo, kicking and splashing as they fought for the ball. It was too rough for me, and besides, I was considered one of the young kids, so I stayed on the sidelines to watch and cheer.

When they'd had enough Richard* challenged me to race him to the float. He was a good swimmer; but so was I, and I took him up on it. We reached it at the same time, well ahead of the rest.

"Man alive, you are some swimmer," he said as we hung on to the ladder catching our breath. "Come here little doll." With that he lunged at me and began rubbing up and down against me. I was more surprised than anything else, and hastily pushed myself away.

Again, I never spoke of it but I began to wonder, what in the world's going on? Why all of a sudden is this happening? Are other girls having the same sort of experience?" I was ashamed and never asked.

Here we were, living in an ideal, safe place—yet I found that even committed Christian men had clay feet. I was disappointed but a little wiser, knowing I would probably have to deal with such behavior in the years ahead.

*Real names not used.

The Camp Meeting

They preach the word of God.
Acts 13:5

Our stay at the beach lasted most of July and August. During that time Daddy took a trip north to Sin Weuiju on the Yalu River to attend the annual revival meeting. The last time I saw him we spent several hours talking about his life and work, and he spoke of one meetings that was different from any of the others.

Arriving in the city after a long hard trip of several days' drive on rough single-track roads, he went straight to the meeting as there was only an hour before the first service was to begin. An elder from the Presbyterian Church spotted his car and rushed over to greet him.

"*Nam Moksa-nim,*" (Honorable Pastor Lampe) he said, "you have arrived just in time. You must preach tonight because Kang Moksa is ill. He has lost his voice. He can't even whisper!"

"How can I preach?" Daddy protested. "I'm not prepared; I'm dirty, tired and hot. Isn't there somebody else who can take over?"

"*Moksa-nim,*" the elder pleaded, "there is nobody else to deliver the sermon."

"Please give me the scripture and the topic. I will think and pray while I clean up." If he hurried, there was time.

A huge crowd of thousands would be there in an outdoor gathering, but Daddy had a fine speaking voice and could be heard clearly even without a mike. When he began to preach, he felt a power take hold of him that was not his own. At times he lost track of what he was saying. It was almost as if he were standing aside, watching himself preach! He didn't understand it, but he just let it happen. He was aware that the Holy Spirit was using him in a direct, unhindered way. When the meeting ended many came forward to confess Jesus Christ as Lord and surrender their lives to Him.

"*Nam Moksanim,*" said those who knew Daddy well, "that was not you speaking tonight. The language you used was our language mixed in with Chinese. You used words you don't even know!"

Daddy had been preaching in Korea for years and saw many converted to Jesus. Yet as he recounted it to me I could see something was eluding him.

For the last seven years of his life, Daddy lived with my younger sister, Molly, and Harwood, her husband. A great love and respect developed between the two men. Harwood, son of Bishop Sturtevant of Fond du Lac, Wisconsin, spent many hours discussing Christian faith and doctrine with Daddy and was seriously thinking of leaving the practice of medicine to enter the ministry.

During a charismatic renewal at St. James Episcopal Church, Harwood and Molly received the gift of tongues and talked with Daddy about it. He said that he had neither had the gift nor felt the need to ask for it. He was, however, interested in their experience.

Several times Daddy told Harwood about that particular preaching experience. During one of his last days he related it once again. There was still something that he couldn't quite grasp. Sin Weuiju is on the border with Manchuria, so the language of the people has a lot of Chinese mixed in. Although all could understand what Daddy was saying in Korean, that night he spoke their language. The truth of what had happened finally dawned on him.

With tears of joy streaming down his face, he realized he had been speaking in tongues. At the appropriate time, God gave him the gift.

The Wanpaoshan Incident (Manposan)

He will cover you with His pinions, and under His wings you may seek refuge;
His faithfulness is a shield and bulwark.
Ps. 91:4

Foreigners living in Korea were blessed with civil peace and quiet, but our neighbors to the north and west were under constant pressure from bandits and scrapping warlords who kept things stirred up. Missionaries were kidnapped for ransom, some were killed, and others barely escaped with their lives. Home-schooling for the children was constantly disrupted. Although the Japanese were the ones we loved to hate, they maintained peace and order in Korea.

Since tranquillity was the norm, it came as no small surprise in 1931 when we learned of the "Wanpaoshan Incident" (Chinese name) or the "Manposan Incident" (Korean name). Japan was desperate for more food, and several families in the southern provinces of Korea grew the world's best rice. Needing an excuse to relocate them to Manchuria to farm territory they had acquired, the Japanese taxed them to the point where they had to give up their lands and agree to move.

There was just one problem. Rice growing requires a lot of water, and irrigation was controlled by Chinese farmers. Without so much as a by-your-leave or any attempt at negotiation, the Koreans dug a canal across land that was not theirs and diverted water to their fields. The Chinese farmers were furious and dammed up the outlet, but the Koreans immediately reopened it. The controversy continued to build until the Chinese began beating up on the Koreans, and being a much larger group, gave them a rough time. Some were killed. Feeling responsible for their citizens, the Japanese called in guards assigned to the trans-Manchurian Rail Road to protect the Korean farmers.

Always looking for an "incident" to legitimize their expansion into Manchuria, the Japanese made the most of the conflict by publicizing it widely.

"Your brothers have been abused and beaten up in Manchuria by the Chinese," they said. "You good Koreans can settle the score by going after the Chinese living here." And they did. Mobs were encouraged to sack a Chinese farming village on the west side of Pyeng Yang. When police were called for help, they just let the rioters do what they wanted. Several farmers were killed. The owner of Taion & Company, a fine Chinese tailor used by most Americans, fled with his wife and children while his home and shop were looted and burned. A front-page newspaper account included a picture of a man lying on the street in a pool of blood as an armed policeman stood aside, arms folded, doing nothing.

At Sorai Beach, we got only snatches of news as people came from Pyeng Yang or Seoul, but before long the problem was on our doorstep. In nearby Kumipo Village we could only buy fresh vegetables, fruit, fish, and live chickens. Steward (so named because he served as a steward on a ship for many years), a Chinese merchant from Seoul, came each summer to run a store that carried staples. Being Chinese, he was fair game for the mob acting up in Kumipo. The community could not stand by and let him be harmed, so a group of men organized to protect him.

First they tested the only road out. Sure enough, it was blocked with a big felled tree. Men with sticks and a supply of stones were there to stop anyone from leaving. That meant they had to get Steward away by boat. Johnny Bigger, one of the older boys and a good sailor, offered to take him from the beach four miles up the coast to the point where the road ran near the ocean just before it turned inland. A car could pick Steward up and take him to the safety of a police station.

While Dr. Bigger was in Pyeng Yang, Mother went to spend the night with his wife. She was concerned about Johnny's undertaking the mission. If the mob should get hold of them, it could be grim.

Late in the day Steward was brought to the beach, where he boarded the fifteen-foot sailboat along with Johnny and another man. They got the outboard engine going and were but a few hundred yards off shore when it quit. They pulled and pulled without being able to get it started again. There was no wind for sailing, so they kept working on the engine. The Koreans found out about the escape attempt and rushed down to the beach. Commandeering a beached fishing boat, they gathered some rocks and began pushing out into the water. With a couple of men on a fishtail oar, they can make a boat fly. Johnny and the others were in real danger.

Arch Campbell was one of the lookouts. He was a big man with a big reputation. He had survived mauling by a bear that tried to scratch out his eyes and had the scars on his forehead and cheeks to prove it. When he saw what they were up to, he tore down to the beach, grabbed the oar, ran with it up the bluff on the beach side and over to the ocean side. With a mighty heave, he sent it crashing down the cliff to the rocks below. Arch wasn't afraid. No way was anyone going to lay a hand on him!

Before they could think of some other way to catch the escapees, a heavy fog moved in and covered the whole bay. Johnny never did get the engine going, but using paddles they made it to the rendezvous with a car that had gotten past the roadblock.

Daddy did the fresh-food shopping early each morning and was back with a loaded basket before breakfast. The day after the escape he brought an amusing report.

"Quite a few men at the market were nursing hangovers and looking sheepish and ashamed."

The event added a bit of excitement for a few days. Nobody was hurt, and before the end of the summer the whole episode had blown over. Everything was back to normal—swimming, sailing, and taking life easy.

Summer gave us two whole months of absolute bliss. When the rains began and the days turned cooler, we reluctantly washed and stored the curtains and bedding in the two coffins. We bolted storm covers over the windows and fastened down the shutters. When everything was locked up tight we drove away feeling more than a little sad.

But there was school to look forward to and good times with old friends and maybe even some new ones. What a life. To think that some people feel sorry for missionary kids!

Bandits
The Hendersons

. . . and having done all, to stand.
Eccl. 7:26

An uneasy tension existed between foreigners and the Japanese occupiers. There was no question as to who was boss and who were guests. Over time a grudging respect developed for the order maintained under their administration, not the least of which was civil discipline. That was not the case in China, where battles raged between warlords; and bandits, the nucleus of the Communist party, plundered and terrorized the countryside at will. Missionaries could never count on long-term residence except in the major cities, and schools were constantly disrupted. Quite often people fled to Korea for refuge until a local conflict was over.

In the 1930s the Lloyd and Harold Henderson families were both stationed in Taigu in southern Korea. With the increasing Korean population in Manchuria, Lloyd and his wife, Helen, volunteered to set up a new mission there. Although still considered somewhat risky, it was generally safer than it had been, and Lloyd was eager to go.

In October of 1932, Helen stayed with us in Syenchun while her husband went ahead to see what housing was available and to make contact with Korean Christians. He expected to be back in no more than two weeks to take her to their new home. Their two young children, Dorothy and Lawrence, stayed with the Harold Hendersons during that time.

On a remote mountain pass, Lloyd and his party were ambushed by a gang of bandits and shot to death. Shortly thereafter a telegram arrived from the American Consulate General in Seoul. Betty, Jim, and I were slaving away in the schoolroom that glorious fall day. The sun was bright, the air crisp and clean. It seemed a crime to be kept indoors. Aunt Helen was in the sewing room cutting out a dress of beautiful red silk from a pattern in the latest fashion that had just come from the States. The doorbell rang, and a minute later Daddy came up holding a yellow envelope. He had a strange look on his face.

"Ruth, please come here a minute," he said. I'd never heard that tone in his voice; something was terribly wrong. Together they went to the sewing room and gave Aunt Helen the telegram. We stood in the doorway, not making a sound as she read it. Mother took the scissors from her hand and held her in her arms as they both wept. The red dress was never finished.

When we were told what happened, I felt so sorry for Dorothy and Lawrence. They were just a little younger than I, but I remember seeing them at the beach. What would they do now without a daddy, I wondered, and poor Aunt Helen! She was going to be terribly sad without her husband. I was so glad Daddy didn't have to go where it was dangerous.

Though the Manchurian border was fifty miles away, the tragedy of senseless murder entered our home and touched our lives.

The Stams

And falling on his knees he cried out with a loud voice, "Lord, do not hold this sin against them!"
Acts 7: 60

In spite of huge distances separating us from those in the China mission, close ties united us because many of them sent their children to our Pyeng Yang Foreign School. Ruth Bell Graham, (Billy Graham's wife), for example, was in Betty's class. Quite a few families from there came to Sorai Beach for summer vacations. It took seven changes between train, boat, and bus and nine days to get there, but they all felt it was worthwhile.

Betty Scott was the daughter of Presbyterian missionaries in China. Three of her siblings, Beatrice, Francis (in Heydon's class), and Kenneth attended PYFS. After she graduated from Wilson College and the Moody Bible Institute in the States, she went to work with the China Inland Mission. There she married John Stam, also with the CIM.

John and Betty with their infant daughter, Helen Priscilla, had not been long settled in Tsingteh, South Anhwei Province, before the Communists attacked. On December 6, 1934, the town was overrun, and they couldn't escape. John was bound and taken away, and soldiers were sent to fetch Betty and the baby as well.

Resistance was useless with the Communists six thousand strong.

John walked the twelve miles to Miaosheo carrying Helen, not yet three months old; Betty rode on a horse some of the way. Part of their agony was hearing the talk about getting rid of the infant before she could cause trouble. A man who had been released from prison when the Communists overran the town objected to killing a baby surely not worthy of death.

"Then it's your life for hers," was the angry retort.

"I am willing," replied the old farmer. And it is recorded that he was killed on the spot.[1]

That night they were put under guard in an abandoned house with John securely tied to the bedposts. Betty was permitted greater freedom so she could take care of Helen.

Hands tied and wearing only light clothing, early the next morning they were marched in the freezing cold through the town and to the top of a hill. There in a pine grove, John was ordered to his knees. A sword did its work. Betty hesitated a moment before she knelt beside John. Mercifully, she didn't see the blade as it glinted briefly before taking her life, too.

Most of the townspeople fled to the hills. A few at a time returned to see if anything was left of their houses and property. Mr. and Mrs. Lo, friends of the Stams, were stunned to learn of their execution. Finding the frozen bodies on the hill, they bought two coffins, wrapped their friends in cotton cloth, and laid them to rest.

But where was little Helen, they wondered. People were afraid to talk. Though the Communists had left, surely some spies remained. Finally an old woman pointed to a large house and whispered, "The baby is in there." Mr. Lo went and knocked, but there was no answer. He entered and looked around; there was nothing. Just as he was about to leave he heard a sound. Yes, it was the wail of a baby. Hurrying to an inner court, he found her on a bed, still snugly wrapped in her sleeping bag. Thirty hours had

---

[1] *John and Betty Stam: A Story of Triumph*
Taylor, Mrs. Howard, Moody Press

passed since John and Betty had been taken away, yet she looked just fine. Mr. Lo picked her up and took her to his wife, who was able to find a wet nurse to feed her.

The Los had a four-year-old son who became very ill from sleeping out of doors during the days and nights they were hiding from the Communists. It was an urgent matter for them to get both children to safety and under good medical care, but there was a problem. They had lost everything to Communist looters, and they needed money for the hundred-mile trip to the nearest help. Before they were marched to their executions that terrible morning, Betty had pinned two five-dollar bills inside Helen's sleeping bag along with extra diapers and gowns.

On foot and as secretly as possible, Mr. and Mrs. Lo made their escape from Miaosheo, the children hidden in two large rice baskets hanging from the ends of a bamboo carrying pole. They would have had nothing to pay the brave man who undertook to carry the baskets had they not found the provision Betty had made for her baby that last night.

Within weeks Helen was taken to her grandparents, Dr. and Mrs. Scott, who lived in Tsinan until their retirement. A poem by Betty is apropos.

Afraid? [2]

Afraid? Of what?
To feel the spirit's glad release?
To pass from pain to perfect peace,
The strife and strain of life to cease?
Afraid—of that?

Afraid? Of what?
Afraid to see the Savior's face,
To hear His welcome, and to trace
The glory gleam from wounds of grace?
Afraid--of that?

---

[2] Ibid., 117

Afraid? Of what?
A flash, a crash, a pierced heart;
Darkness, light, O Heaven's art!
A wound of His counterpart!
Afraid—of that?

Afraid? Of what?
To do by death what life could not—
Baptize with blood a stony plot,
Til souls shall blossom from the spot?
Afraid—of that?

Dr. and Mrs. Petersen.

Render unto Caesar the things which are Caesar's; and unto God the things that are God's.
Matt. 22:21

Sin Weuiju lies on the Korean side of the Yalu River with Antung opposite on the Manchurian side. Both were just an hour's train ride north of Syenchun. The Petersens were with a Danish mission in Antung, where he established and ran a small hospital on the city's outskirts. Several times a year our parents took a day off to visit them and do a little shopping. There they could purchase small luxuries such as Lux soap, unavailable in Korea.

When bandits were caught, tried, and found guilty, they were sentenced to death. The custom was to place the head of the executed in a basket and hang it from a light post in the marketplace, where everybody could see and take notice. One day a young man, no more than a teenager, was brought to the hospital. He had been wounded and captured during a fight with government forces. The chief of police came to the hospital in person to speak to Dr. Petersen.

"Please, sir, do what you can to restore this man to perfect health. When he is well, he will be tried and shot. His head will be a warning to others. That's the proper end for all bandits."

After surgery, medication, and a lot of TLC, the boy began to heal and gain strength. They posted a guard at his door to make sure he didn't escape, and every day a police officer checked on his progress.

The law was the law, but Dr. Petersen also knew that many times young men had no choice in the matter. When bandit gangs needed more recruits, they raided a village, held pistols to the heads of men with children, and threatened to blow their brains out if they didn't give one or more of their sons to the gang. The young men had to go.

This particular lad was only sixteen and seemed like such a nice youngster. The day before he was to be turned over to the police, Dr. Petersen stopped by his room late in the afternoon.

"You've done very well," he said, "and you're about ready to leave the hospital. Just thought I'd mention that the guard outside your door goes off duty at 10:00 p.m., and the door at the end of the hall is left unlocked all night." The next morning it was discovered that the bandit had escaped.

Several weeks later the Petersens were awakened in the middle of the night by a loud pounding on their front door.

"We have a wounded man who needs your attention right away," a voice shouted.

All evening there had been sporadic small-arms fire in the distance but no more than usual. Dr. Petersen put on his robe and slippers, reached for his bag, and went downstairs to admit two men carrying a wounded man on a stretcher. They put him down on the living room floor. As Dr. Petersen leaned over to turn back the blanket, they pounced on him, bound and gagged him, put him on the stretcher, and carried him off.

Within a few days word came that the bandits were demanding thousands of rounds of ammunition and great sums of money for his release. The Danish mission, however, had a firm policy of paying no ransom, ever. When the bandits realized they wouldn't get any, they began to lessen their demands, though still threatening to harm or kill the doctor. The Danes stood firm in their resolve.

Soon Mrs. Petersen began receiving messages saying she could send personal items to her husband. She was to leave packages in designated places for pickup. Each time she got a message she responded with food, seasonable clothing, and whatever medicine she thought he might be able to use. In the middle of the night six weeks later, he walked into the house.

"The bandits knew I didn't approve of the way they lived, but at least they were confident I wasn't against them after I saved the life of one of their men," he said in telling of this experience. "They carried me everywhere in a green sedan chair. I've seen parts of China I never would have seen any other way, and I've experienced their life. It gave me an opportunity to demonstrate love and concern when they brought me their sick, and I found that many were interested in hearing about my Jesus as well. Except for the worry it caused family and friends, I regret none of it. Those were the best days of my missionary life!"

Two years later the Petersens returned to Denmark, but before leaving they gave us Lexie, a beautiful little fox terrier. She became the eleventh member of our family.

The Other Side of the Border

Thou wilt keep him in perfect peace, whose mind is stayed on thee; because he trusteth in Thee.

Is. 26:3

Daddy's territory covered four provinces along the Yalu River: Pyuktong, Changsung, Sakchu, and Weuiju. Some of the area was so mountainous it had to be traveled on foot. Though Korea was comparatively safe, the border was not guarded except at railroad stations and major bridges. Anyone could cross in a small boat and go unchallenged. It happened frequently.

During one of Daddy's journeys across rugged terrain, he and his Korean helper were walking through a narrow pass when suddenly they were surrounded by two hundred hostile men. They had no weapons that Daddy could see, but the way they stood blocking the road, the clenched fists, and their hard faces told him what they had in mind. Their clothing indicated they were from the other side of the border. Although Daddy was well aware of what bandits did to missionaries, he had no sense of fear.

"Please stand aside," he said, walking up to the leader and looking him in the eye. "My friend and I are going through." Without argument, the bandits parted to let them pass. "We never looked back, nor did we hurry; but it was a great relief to reach the next village."

Quite a few Koreans lived on the Manchurian side of the Yalu River. There were five small churches over there, but none had a pastor. Time and again the congregations sent word to Daddy, begging him to come help them, but whenever he seriously considered going, everyone strenuously pleaded with him not to. It simply wasn't safe. The urgent requests continued until he finally decided he had to go in spite of the strong arguments against it.

"If you must go, I'll go with you," said Mr. Lee, an elder Daddy knew well.

They started with the four churches just north of the river. All was quiet during their two-day visit, and the meetings went well. The remaining church, however, was farther inland. Mr. Lee, himself, tried to talk Daddy out of visiting that one. It was a good ten-mile walk, the roads were muddy, and more rain threatened. It could be very dangerous.

"I appreciate the problems," Daddy said, "but we've come this far, so why not finish the job? They insist that they need me. Let's go."

"All right, but you must promise me one thing," Mr. Lee said. "Keep your eyes down if we should meet anybody, and don't smile; don't open your mouth or say a word, not one. I will do all the talking." Daddy agreed.

They passed several villages, each with armed guards at the gates. Speaking Chinese, which Daddy didn't understand, Mr. Lee seemed to know what to say. They were not hindered in any way. He apparently knew some of the guards with whom he joked and laughed. They reached the church before dark, held the meeting, and spent the night there before returning to the Yalu River by a different route.

After they had safely crossed into Korea, Daddy turned to his friend and asked, "Now tell me, what was all that about?"

"You see," Mr. Lee answered, "I was once a bandit. Before I was converted I lived over there. I know the villages, and a few of the guards at the gates were old buddies of mine. When I asked to pass, they wanted to know what I was doing with a foreign devil. I told them you were my prisoner, and I was taking you to another village, where I'd have a little sport with you before I killed you; so they let us go!"

Uncle Tom Winn

Days should speak, and multitude of years should teach wisdom.
Job 32:7

After Daddy graduated from Knox College in Galesburg, Illinois, he spent two years in Japan teaching English. He wanted to learn for himself if he had the disposition to work with Asians. One of the major attractions was that Lila Winn, his mother's sister, and her husband, Thomas, were in Japan with the Presbyterian mission. After working with them, he returned to the States, attended Omaha Theological Seminary, and then accepted a call to pastor a small church in Ponca, Nebraska, for two years. It was there he met Mother, the prettiest girl in the choir.

Daddy applied to the Presbyterian Board of Foreign Missions for an appointment to Japan, but his application was refused. The U.S. government was not pleased with that country's aggression in Korea. Instead he agreed to go to Korea, a decision he never regretted, though he was sorry not to be serving with his Uncle Tom.

After seven years Mother and Daddy left for their first stateside furlough with Heydon, Willard, and Cordelia. The journey from Syenchun was long and exciting. First came the twenty-hour train ride to Pusan, then the overnight ferry to Shimonosaki, followed by another train to Yokohama to catch the ship for Seattle or San Francisco. There was one more train to their home.

They broke the trip with a visit to Uncle Tom and Aunt Lila in Kanazawa. At an appropriate moment, Aunt Lila took Mother aside to have a "little talk."

"Ruth, you have three beautiful, healthy children. Don't you think it would be best to limit your family so you can devote more time to supporting Henry in his work?" she asked.

Mother and Daddy must have thought about it, but not too seriously, as they produced another little Lampe every two years or so until there were eight of us.

Uncle Tom and Aunt Lila had a fine ministry in Japan. They arrived in 1874 when they were expecting their first baby and were the first white people to cross Lake Biwa. They were shipwrecked in a bad storm and lost all the baby's equipment—a potential disaster. Living for a time in a Buddhist temple, they made do with what was available in the market and finally settled in Kanazawa.

Tom preached on street corners in the snow (a lot of it) and founded a church and a school for training young women in kindergarten arts. He brought alfalfa to Japan and went by horseback to Eddo (Tokyo during the Meiji period) to plead for a railway to northern Japan so fishermen could sell their catch in cities. In later years the government gave him a ride along the whole length of their railroad system as a reward. A very practical man, he introduced the first toothbrush and built the first motorbike seen in Japan. He was a forceful person who knew what he wanted and frequently laid down the law to his wife. One Saturday evening he retired to his study to prepare a sermon for the next day.

"I am not to be disturbed for any reason," he announced. "I have work to do and cannot see anybody, no matter who he may be." The words were no more than out of his mouth when a young man knocked at the door.

"What may I do for you?" Aunt Lila asked.

"I want to learn how to make chocolate cookies, chocolate

cake, and chocolate candy," he stated.

"Dr. Winn cannot be disturbed," she explained, but that did not discourage her caller.

"I wait," he said. Hour after hour passed with no sign that Uncle Tom had finished his sermon. "Wouldn't it be better to come back another day?" she urged.

"I wait." At ll:00 p.m. she tapped timidly at the study door.

"I said I was not to be disturbed! Can I have no peace? What in the world is the matter?" She told him about the little man who wouldn't go away. He went storming out to where the guest waited.

"What is it you want at this hour of the night?" he demanded.

Unabashed, the visitor repeated his request.

"So," Tom bellowed, "We'd better get started." Lila fled to the bedroom to pray and sleep while the two men spent most of the night cooking.

Who was that young man? Mr. Morinaga, one of the many Uncle Tom taught, housed, and brought to the Lord. He became one of Japan's largest manufacturers of chocolate confections. His trademark is a circle enclosing a large *M.* held by a downward-flying, fat little cherub.

After forty years of service the Winns retired In 1930 but elected to stay in Japan. His answer to the Presbyterian Mission Board when they asked him to come home was, "Come and get me."

Tom and Lila had many friends all over Japan, Korea, and China, and to visit them they took the Grand Tour—by ship to Pusan and train up the length of Korea and through China, down to Hong Kong, and ship again back to Japan. One of their stops was in Syenchun to see us.

"They arrived on one of those golden days when everything was perfect," Mother said, recalling the event. "The weather was just right, and all of the children behaved; they didn't scrap or spill food at the table and were polite!" When all were safely tucked in bed, the four adults sat down to talk. "Lila," Mother asked with a twinkle in her eye, "which ones would you have me drown?"

"Oh, Ruth, I did hope you had forgotten that conversation," she answered, covering her face with both hands.

Lila spent an hour or more in prayer before going to bed. One night Tom found her there on her knees, but she was dead. She died as she had lived, praying.

Several years later Tom was feeling unwell one Sunday morning but didn't want to take a rickshaw. With his sermon in his pocket, he walked to the church, which was celebrating its fiftieth anniversary. He went down the aisle and sat on a front seat to pray before going up to the pulpit. During the hymn before his sermon, he collapsed and died, falling onto the arm of a lady seated next to him. She later reported that she felt blessed.

Their eldest son, George, a missionary in Korea, was asked to preach at the funeral service a week later. He used the sermon Tom had in his pocket, all written out in *romaji* (English letters). The topic was "Eternal Life."

The Japanese church undertook all expenses for the funeral, burial plot, and headstone and decorated the graves with flowers all during World War II. Because of his great contributions, Tom was declared a national treasure.

Paul Winn, Tom's grandson, was a missionary in China during the war. After his capture in Ningpo he was held under house-arrest for two years. On December 7, 1941, he was taken by ship to Shanghai, where he was put into Bridgehouse Concentration Camp. All new prisoners were tried in a kangaroo court. As his father had counseled him, he attempted to warn several U.S. soldiers who were housed with him.

"Be sure to answer 'guilty' when you are brought before a military judge, no matter what the charge. It's the only way you'll survive," he said. They refused to do so and one by one were taken out and shot.

Finally it was Paul's turn to be tried as a civilian accused of espionage. When confronted with the charge, he smiled and answered in the affirmative.

"Winn?" asked the secretary-translator, "Do you know our

Thomas Winn?"

"I am the first son of the first son of Thomas Winn, who lived in Kanazawa," Paul answered. The secretary, who had been one of Tom's students of English, asked for a recess. He wrote out Tom's contributions to Japan. After considering the message, the judge passed sentence: Life imprisonment.

"Hallelujah!" Paul said, knowing the United States would win the war, and he'd soon be released.

"What did he say?" the judge asked.

"He is very happy," reported the secretary. So Paul was not tortured as were all other prisoners.

"You know," Paul told us some years later, "the Bible says that the blessings of the father will be passed along to the children to the third and fourth generation. Well, I just slipped through."

Under Japanese Rule

Let every person be in subjection to the governing authorities.
For there is no authority except from God,
and those which exist are established by God.
Rom. 13:1-2

Japan ruled Korea from the early 1900s to the end of World War II. Some things they did were good. In addition to the railroad they constructed roads, established law and order, built schools, and permitted freedom of worship.

But there is no substitute for freedom, and the Koreans hated them. Little manufacturing was developed. Raw materials were shipped to Japan and the finished goods sold abroad. Koreans weren't permitted to hold top positions but were assigned mid- and low-level jobs, and absolutely no political dissent was tolerated.

It wasn't long before students in Christian colleges began to see the injustice of it all and protested. The Japanese came to regard mission schools as training ground for the opposition, and that was certainly the case. Syngman Rhee, the first president of South Korea, was one of them. He fled to Hawaii many years before Korea gained her independence because outspoken critics of Japan often ended up in prison; others had "unfortunate accidents."

Early in his ministry, Daddy's attitude was formed by the lessons he found in the New Testament. The Jews lived under Roman domination. They hated it and longed for the day they would be free. Yet what was Jesus' attitude? He urged all to honor those in authority, obey the law, and pay their taxes. How could the missionaries do any less?

One way to keep the peace and stay in the good graces of Japanese authorities was by giving gifts at appropriate times. We had a garden that provided fruits and vegetables for our large family. At the beginning of the season, strawberries are at their biggest and best. Each year Mother sent a basket to the chief of police with Daddy's calling card. One year they were out of town when the first berries were harvested, but as soon as possible upon their return Mother sent the annual offering. The berries were a little smaller than usual. Through the bamboo wireless it was made known that the chief was not pleased to have missed the "first fruits" of the strawberry crop. I don't think Mother lost any sleep over it.

Even the U.S. government took part in the effort to maintain good relations. On a special birthday of the emperor's daughter, the American consulate in Seoul sent a stunning doll to each city where our citizens were located. They were gifts to the daughters of the local chiefs of police. Betty Campbell was chosen to be the presenter for our station. During the ceremony we sat on one side of the room and the Japanese on the other. After tea and speeches, Betty met the recipient in the center of the room. The girls bowed to each other, and Betty gave her the doll. It was the most beautiful one I'd ever seen, one that any of us would have died for.

In the late 1930s Japanese authority grew intrusive and tiresome. Annual car inspections were extremely detailed and thorough. They tolerated no defect, no matter how minor. The driving test was equally tough. The candidate had to maneuver both forward and in reverse without hitting any of the marker pegs driven into the ground in a tight figure eight.

The hassle didn't end there. Gasoline was strictly rationed. There were no service stations. It had to be purchased from a specific dealer in five-gallon tins. If Daddy had a trip up country, a good share of his trunk space was taken up with gas, and on one of extended duration, he had to get written permission to buy more. The regulations seemed to be endless; but there was no choice, and they were followed to the letter.

Daddy had a .22. Each year an officer appeared at our door to inspect the rifle and collect a tax. Broken down, it was stored on one of the upper shelves in Daddy's office closet. He used it so infrequently that I wonder why he kept it. The only time I remember seeing him shoot was when we had suckling pig for a big station dinner. The day before, a baby pig was hung by its hind legs from the laundry line in the back yard. As it squealed and wiggled around, Daddy shot it right in the heart. It died instantly. Tin Hoop-i cut its throat to let all the blood run out. It was gutted, scalded, scraped, and washed before going to the kitchen.

All day long the house was filled with the smell of roasting pork. When the golden brown piglet was finally presented at the table with cherries for eyes and an apple in its mouth, I lost my appetite. All I could think about was that poor little animal and the dreadful things that had been done to it.

After the Japanese invaded Manchuria and the coastal cities of China in 1937, they were anxious that Koreans not give them any trouble and tried harder than ever to make them loyal to Emperor Hirohito. All were required to take Japanese surnames, and instruction in school was in Japanese. Koreans were supposed to speak only Japanese, even in their homes; but of course it didn't happen. There was no way to enforce such a law.

Foreigners were more carefully watched. For two years I took a seven-hour train trip every other weekend from boarding school in Pyeng Yang to Seoul to the orthodontist to have my braces adjusted. Each time I entered the station a plainclothesman (we called him Mr. Brown because he always wore a brown suit) approached with notebook in hand and a short stub of a pencil. "Excuse please. What ees-a your name?" I gave it and answered the usual questions.

"Where are you going? How long you stay? What train you return? Sank you velly much." With a toothy smile and a nod he was off to find other traveling foreigners. Indeed they did have a good record of wherever we went. I ached to give Mr. Brown some wrong information to see what would happen, but I didn't dare.

Since the Japanese claimed their emperor was descended from the Sun Goddess, certain parts of the Book of Revelation were offensive to them. Several passages contradicted their belief that the line of their goddess would never end, so Christians were asked not to preach from the offending text. Plainclothesmen attended most worship services, but Daddy maintained it didn't bother him at all. "I'm eager to see the conversion of Koreans and Japanese alike," he said.

Every time he took a trip out of town, he was required to report it to the chief of police in Syenchun. One night after a long hard drive through heavy rain on a miserable, one-lane, rutted road, he was stopped just before entering the town by a policeman and told to go back ten lee (about five miles) to police headquarters. "The chief wants to see you." Although he was already late, there was nothing to do but turn around and go back.

"Is there something you wish to say to me?" Daddy inquired when he reached the station.

"Dr. Lampe," the chief answered, "you have been in this area a long time. People love you and believe you, so I ask that you be very careful about what you say."

"Thank you very much. I'll be careful," Daddy promised and was on his way. How strange that such a wonderful compliment should come from an enemy officer.

In a desperate effort to gain Korean loyalty, the Japanese gave an order that all schools must take their students out to the Shinto shrine on certain days and bow to the east to honor Emperor Hirohito. It was published in the papers and broadcast on the radio that it was not an act of worship but simply a way of showing honor to the emperor, rather like saluting the flag.

It brought immediate strong protest from Christian schools and colleges. Many decided to close rather than obey. Others wondered how to handle it. Christian education was making a profound difference in Korea, so should they close the schools or try to live with the latest rule? These were hard choices.

A number of outspoken missionaries were warned to watch it. What was Daddy's position? He wasn't out there making public statements, so what did he think?

"Quite a few Korean pastors came to me asking for help," he told us later. After much prayer and meditation he gave an answer typical of the godly man he was. "I reminded them that they were no longer babies in the faith. 'Because you have grown up, matured, and are on the solid food of the Word, I'll not tell you what to do. I am not asked to go to the shrine, so it's not something I must decide; but you must. If you believe you can accept the government's statement that it's just a patriotic act, go. If you can't, if you believe in your heart that it is an act of heathen worship, you should be willing to die rather than go. It is up to you. God will judge you according to your lights."

A good answer? I thought so, but if you listened to the judgment of some of the other missionaries, you'd have been certain Daddy was on the fast track to hell. It was awful what some of them said, but in his own words, "Each will be judged by the Father who knows our hearts." Amen, Lord, and thank you.

Daddy, that good lookin' man

The Little Boxes

There is an appointed time for everything, and there is a time for every event under heaven—A time to give birth, and a time to die.

Eccl. 3:1-2a.

At Sorai Beach all was quiet that summer of 1937, yet we wondered about the warships that appeared on the horizon, silhouetted against the western sky. They stayed a few days then vanished in the night. More appeared—battleships, heavy cruisers, and gunboats.

In that remote resort where we had neither electricity nor running water, we could only speculate on their significance until someone arrived from Seoul with newspapers telling of Japan's invasion of the coastal cities of China. The military faction in Japan had won out and the first shots of World War II fired.

Preparing for war, the Japanese had built a two-track railway the length of Korea. They shipped troops overnight from Japan to the port of Pusan at the southern tip of the country, loaded them on trains, and in less than twenty-four hours delivered them to the Manchurian front.

In every movie theater newsreels depicted one great Japanese victory after another. First they bombarded a city then mounted a charge against any fortifications it might have. Their victorious soldiers strutted atop the ancient walls, arms raised, rifles in hand, shouting, *"Bonzai, bonzai."*

On my trips to the orthodontist in Seoul, I'd frequently see a troop train in the station about to head north with a load of new recruits. Japanese women in kimonos and aprons went up and down the platform with trays of tea, cookies, and fruit. Young soldiers in their brand new uniforms reached eagerly for the gifts. They laughed and posed for pictures taken by their buddies. As the stationmaster signaled their departure with several blasts on his whistle, they boarded the train and rushed to the windows, hanging out as far as they could, waving little paper flags and shouting jubilantly. There were so many, so young, so eager.

Then I began to see another kind of ceremony. This time the train was headed south, returning from the front. It was filled with little wooden boxes, each carefully wrapped in a white *furoshsiki*, a square of material with opposite corners tied in a knot at the top. They held the ashes of soldiers killed in battle that were being returned to their families in Korea and Japan.

Covered with a white cloth, a card table stood on the platform beside the train. The little boxes were stacked on it. When all was ready, an officer in full-dress uniform stepped down. Several couples approached quietly with downcast eyes. They simply waited.

I wondered what they were thinking and feeling. If it was a son, was his mother remembering the day she first held him in her arms and the joy she felt? Did she stroke his cheeks and trace the curve of his perfect little ear with the tip of her finger as he nursed at her breast? Did she open his tiny hands and ponder what they would do as he grew to manhood? Over the years did she laugh with him as he learned to walk, talk, and play? And what of his father? Was this a son that filled his heart with pride and joy who would carry on the family name? And if there were no other sons, was his line cut short? Were they Christians? Did they have the hope of seeing him again in heaven? My heart ached as I thought of the many who would be facing their loss.

As their names were called they came forward, bowed deeply, and accepted the box with both hands, bowed again, and returned to their places. None showed a trace of emotion.

When the last box had been received, the officer saluted smartly and reboarded the train. The families left, carrying what remained of a son, brother, or husband. An orderly removed the cloth, folded the table and put it back on board. The train with its sad cargo moved slowly out of the station.

The Whan-Gop

With a long life I will satisfy him,
and let him behold My salvation.
Ps. 91:16

September 28, 1938, was Daddy's *Whan-Gop*, a very special day. He was sixty years old. He had completed his Golden Cycle of five times the Chinese rotation of twelve years. According to Asians, from this date forward he'd be living on borrowed time.

It was a big celebration. Daddy received every kind of gift from Korean friends and church groups—bolts of hand-woven silk, brass bowls, silver chopsticks and spoons, fruits, nuts, and sweets. All week long lavish feasts celebrated his special day.

The five older children were in America, but Mother was anxious that Jim, Molly, and I come home from boarding school for the weekend to experience part of the festivities. We received permission from the principal to leave right after our last class on Friday. It was going to be a rush to make it to the express train, so Jim offered to purchase the tickets the weekend before. I gave him the money, thanked him for his help, and thought nothing more of it.

We were excited about the prospect of going home as we rushed to the dorms for our bags. Cramming them and ourselves into the tiniest taxi you ever saw (one of the first Datsons), we headed for the station.

"I guess I should have told you, Fran, but I don't have the tickets," Jim said as we pulled up at the station. I couldn't believe my ears.

"What do you mean, you don't have the tickets?" I demanded.

"Well," he said, "on the way to the station Saturday I saw some really pretty little Japanese lanterns made of bronze with tiny electric lights in them. I thought they would be a good present for Mary and Heydon for Christmas, so I bought them. I thought they'd look nice on their mantelpiece. I forgot to tell you."

"How could you forget such a thing?" I was completely dumbfounded. The train was in the station ready to go, and I had no money. Mother was counting on our being there for dinner. I was ready to kill him! The only thing I could think of was to ask help from a perfect stranger. The tickets had to be purchased in the next two minutes, or we'd miss the train. There was no time for planning strategy; I had to act immediately. Express trains ran on time and didn't wait for anybody.

"Excuse me, sir," I said, to the ticket agent "I have a problem. I asked my younger brother to buy three express tickets to Syenchun last Saturday, but he spent the money on a gift, so now we can't get on the train that is in the station right now. Everybody will be so sad if we miss my father's sixtieth birthday celebration. Please, is there any way you could help us? "

Smiling and nodding, he reached into his pocket, pulled out several bills, put them in the cash drawer, and handed me the tickets. "Have good time wit mudder and fadder," he said "Now hully, hully."

Taking the tickets with both hands and bowing deeply, I thanked him and called over my shoulder as we ran for the gate, "We'll be back Sunday night, and I'll repay you then."

Once safely on the train, I relented a little on wanting to kill my brother. We were living in times of growing scarcity. The Japanese had started their war with China the year before, and all luxury items were fast disappearing. The thinking was, if you see something you're sure you want, buy it. Tomorrow it'll be gone.

Heydon and Mary's wedding had been a big event in our family the month before. It was the very first in our generation, and all of us thought it was wonderful and romantic. Jim wanted to buy something very special for their first Christmas. He saw the lamps as being a perfect gift and felt he had to buy them right away.

The Japanese authorities gave us a few problems, but they were very hard on the Koreans, particularly any who showed leadership potential. We didn't feel kindly toward the oppressors. Nevertheless, Mother was pleased and thankful for the ticket agent's kindness. She not only gave me money to return to him, but a large box of cakes, cookies, and fruit as well. He saved the day, bless his heart, even though he was one of the despised Japanese.

Paik-si Wei-run

Strength and dignity are her clothing, and she smiles at the future.
She opens her mouth in wisdom, and the teaching of kindness is on her tongue.
She looks well to the ways of her household,
and does not eat the bread of idleness.
Her children rise up to bless her.
Prov. 31:25-28a

"We're having a special treat tonight," Mother announced at lunch. "We've been invited to Paik-si's house for dinner, and you children are included. She's a very special person, so I have asked her to tell you her story."

We had been to Korean dinners before, and they were fun. Sitting cross-legged on cushions on the floor around a table and using chopsticks was our idea of a dining experience. Even if the host was not wealthy, course after course appeared on the table. Some dishes were tastier than others, but one thing we could count on—there would be a lot more offered than we could eat. Paik-si was Mother's Bible woman[1] and by any standard, very rich; it would surely be a tremendous feast.

After serving small cups of tea, Paik-si seated us, offered the blessing, and the food began to arrive. We were each given a covered brass bowl of steaming rice and a little tray of condiments to eat with the various dishes we chose. A dish of *kimchi*, hot

[1] A Bible woman was a church member in good standing who had passed the required courses at the Bible Institute. She was an authorized Bible teacher.

and spicy pickled turnip and cabbage, was shared by each two diners. I had my first taste of octopus tentacles, thinly sliced, dipped in beaten egg, and fried—truly good! Chicken and fish came in several forms, along with stir-fried chopped vegetables, beef *pul-kogi* cooked at the table, and *sin-su-lo*, much like Mongolian hot pot, with meat-filled dumplings, vegetables, and chestnuts all bubbling together in a thin chicken broth. It was superb, but even better was Paik-si's story. Mother wanted us to know of her life, and it was best learned from the source. She began while we ate.

"I was just fifteen when my mother and father arranged my marriage to a man twelve years older than I. He was a good man, and his family had many rice lands and a lot of money. Not only were they wealthy, but they had great influence in the community and were highly respected.

"My well-educated husband could read and write Chinese characters and was very wise for his years. After our wedding we spent the traditional one month with my family before moving to a suite of rooms in his family's home. I did not suffer the usual trials of a new bride at the hands of my mother-in-law because my father-in-law obtained an appointment for my husband in Seoul as an advisor to Kojong, the last king of Korea. My husband was the second son and did not have the duty of the first son to live with his parents and take care of them in their old age (Asian Social Security). Before leaving, my husband hired a caretaker to oversee the planting and harvesting of the fields assigned to him.

"All our household goods were packed and loaded onto fifty ponies, and we departed in great style, riding in covered chairs. My third aunt and ten servants came with us. The trip took many days, and our nights were spent at inns that were uncomfortable; but I was young, and the adventure was more than I had ever dreamed of.

"In Seoul my handsome husband bought a nice house for us near the king's palace and found several servants to help take care of our domestic needs. I couldn't have been happier, and before long I was pregnant.

"I didn't know anything about God, so I worshipped as did my husband's family in Syenchun. Wanting to be a good wife and make sure our household prospered, I asked my aunt to help me set up a little shrine at the entrance of the house. We also hung a giving-basket near the ceiling in the main room to appease the spirits.

"But my joy didn't last. Soon after our little son was born, my husband became very ill. He was terribly sick with a high fever and chills and could eat nothing, not even soup. Oh, how frightened I was! I called in everybody I could find to help, but they just shook their heads and went away. On the sixth day he died.

"I was numb with grief, but my aunt knew what to do. The servants had a mourning dress and head covering made for me out of rough hemp. A shaman was called to conduct the funeral, and a man with special powers was engaged to find a suitable burial place. I wanted to be absolutely sure the coffin was placed in just the right direction so that his soul would rest well and he would have a nice view.

"I shall never forget how hard the day of the funeral was. We had a shrine set up in the courtyard with food for the spirits arranged on tables in ornamental designs. Hired mourners came, also dressed in rough hemp. Several people were assigned to help me during the ritual to show me when to bow, sit, or cry.

"My heart felt like a stone in my chest, and my head ached with throbbing pain as we walked to the hill outside the city. It took eight men to carry the large coffin on two long poles. They were followed by the mourners who screamed, cried, and pulled their hair. They did a good job and were paid well because I wanted my husband's spirit to know that his dying was a great sadness to his loving wife. Always there were helpers on either side to assist me as I followed the coffin that terrible day.

When the coffin had been positioned exactly right at the grave, they lit a fire to burn lots of fake money and other things my husband would need in his next life. I didn't approve of it, but I kept my feelings to myself. I had my own ideas about providing for my husband. I didn't want to cheat the man who had been so good to me, so much to the horror of the others, I burned thirty thousand dollars' worth of precious amber. It was the least I could do.

"As soon as possible I arranged for our return to Syenchun. My husband's rice lands now belonged to me and needed to be managed. No hireling could do a better job of it than I.

"At that time I was searching for important answers in my life. The gods worshipped by my family had not brought me peace, but where could I turn? I began to see an order with things in nature. There were the seasons—a time for planting and a time for harvest. Surely there was a god that made the rice to grow, so when I became troubled about something, I went into the shed behind the house and knelt down in front of the rice *toke* to pray. When I did that, things seemed to go well.

"One day when I was in the market somebody handed me a bright piece of paper with some words printed on it. I tucked the message up my sleeve to examine when I got home. It told about a man named Jesus who could answer all my questions, and since he was God, everybody could reach Him. That was a whole new idea. I was invited to come to hear more about this Jesus at a place they called a *quo-whei* (church).

"I began to have new hope and went there every Sunday morning and Wednesday evening. My heart was warmed by what I heard."

We had all been silent as Paik-si spoke. The servants quietly removed empty serving bowls and brought in new courses. Once in a while she pointed to an empty tea cup, and a servant filled it.

"Now comes the best part of the story, so listen carefully," Mother said before Paik-si continued.

"My brother-in-law was very jealous of how well my lands were producing. His were not. He spent too much time at the drinking house and not enough managing the fields. He wanted to take over my land, and one day he came to threaten me.

"I understand you are going to the *quo-whei* these days. You must stop. Crude, dirty people go there, but you are of a high-class family and must not disgrace us,' he said.

"My brother-in-law was a mean fellow who tried to frighten me. We were in the courtyard at the time. He selected a large kitchen knife and began whetting it on a stone as he spoke.

'You see how sharp this is? I can make it even sharper, and if you don't quit going to that place, I'll come and cut your throat. Do you understand?' With a hard thrust he stuck the knife into a post, gave me an evil look, and left. I was terrified and didn't know what to do. I was all alone with the baby, and that terrible man could come into the house any time he chose. I ran out to the shed and prayed: O God who makes the rice to grow, please take my brother-in-law away. The very next day the police arrested him because he was active in the Mansei Movement.[2] At least for a time I would be free of him. I must say I was surprised and thankful that God had heard my prayer. At another time I received a tract saying we should cover ourselves with the Word of God. I was not sure what that meant, but soon after that my little boy became very ill. I was not yet a believer and not completely trusting of missionary doctors. I didn't trust our native medicine people either. Remembering what the paper said, I took a wheelbarrow and went to the marketplace to buy Bibles, all I could manage, and went home. My son was so sick he couldn't even cry. I put him down on the floor and I made sure every part of him was covered with Bibles; then I ran out to the shed and once more knelt to pray. O God that makes the rice to grow, please heal my child. I have covered him with the Word of God. Please make him well.

"The baby was very quiet and seemed to be sleeping, so I left him just as he was, beneath all the Bibles. In a little while he began to move, so I picked him up. The fever was gone. He was smiling and very hungry.

That day as I was preparing rice, I held a grain in my hand. This rice is alive, I thought; if I plant it, it will grow. Then I broke the grain with my fingernail, seeing that I could take life away

---

[2] The Mansei Movement was Korean protest of the Japanese takeover of their country in 1905.

from the rice, but I couldn't give it. Whoever does so is greater than I, and he must be the God I will worship.

"From that time on I was a believer in the Christian God. I bowed my head and asked Jesus to forgive my sins and come into my heart to live there the rest of my days."

I was deeply touched by Paik-si's story and gave thanks that she was the one who went with Mother on her mission trips to the country.

Paik-si's later years were as exciting as her early ones. When Korea was divided and the North was taken over by Communists, the first to be eliminated were the landowners, particularly those who had prospered. And with two hundred families working her lands, Paik-si had done very well.

"I was brought before a court and accused of abuse and neglect of my employees, many of whom came forward to tell of my cruelty and greed. The judgment was that I be put to death and my land divided among them. The sentence was to be carried out the next day. Just as the soldiers were about to lead me away, a young man broke from the ranks of the troops watching the trial. He bowed before the senior officer and asked to be heard.

"I am a loyal Communist soldier," he said. "All my life I have lived on that woman's land (pointing at me) and I have seen my family suffer while she kept all profits for herself and gave us nothing! She is a greedy old woman. It would give me the greatest pleasure to kill her with my own hands, to feel the life go out of her body as I squeeze her neck! Please, sir, will you give me the privilege?"

Wanting to make a good impression on the spectators, the officer agreed. 'Sure, take her. Spill the blood of this filthy capitalist! You have earned it,' he said.

"I recognized my accuser. He was born on the farm, and all of his family were fine Christians. He knew I took good care of all my workers and paid them far more than the usual wage. I wondered what had changed him.

"He picked up the end of the rope that bound my hands and

gave it such a jerk I almost fell. He added a couple of kicks and yanked my hair, cursing me all the way.

'I'm so sorry," he said when we were out of sight,' but I had to do that to get you released to me. I have seen them do it before—they don't like to dirty their own hands. Hurry now, we'll carry on the game until we get away, then I'll see you safely across the border to the south.'"

Sitting in Mother and Daddy's living room in South Korea after they had returned to serve out their years in Korea, she said, "And here I am in your house once again, *Nam pueen-nim*. I have nothing but the clothes I wear, but soon I'll be receiving help from my son. If he wishes, I will visit him and his American wife in Philadelphia. He is a doctor, you know."

Paik-si did go to the States but was happier and more content living and working in Seoul. She died in 1948 and was buried on the hillside next to her husband.

Mother, the Missionary

. . . I call to remembrance the unfeigned faith that . . . dwelt . . . in thy mother.
II Tim. 1:5

When I arrived at Knox College in the fall of 1940, Heydon helped get my suitcases into my room on the third floor of Whiting Hall and left me to settle in. After so many years in boarding school, it was no big deal. I was soon out meeting other freshmen and finding my way around. Several girls from nearby rooms approached me.

"Are you a missionary?" they asked.

"No, but I'm the daughter of one," I answered. They laughed. With my blond hair and clothes like their own, I didn't fit the picture. They all contributed ideas of how they imagined I'd look.

"We thought your hair would be parted in the middle, with two long braids hanging down your back," Audrey announced.

"And you'd use no makeup and probably have buck teeth," Mary added. Meg thought surely I would be wearing lisle stockings and brown Oxford shoes.

"Missionary!" What kind of picture comes to mind when you hear that word? Do you see somebody with tightly drawn back hair, a severe expression, glasses, no jewelry, a long skirt, and sleeves on a dress buttoned up to the neck? Perhaps that description fits some, but not my mother. She was petite, nicely rounded but not fat, and had soft brown hair. True, she wore glasses and only light makeup, but she had a twinkle in her eye, a ready smile, and a happy disposition that drew people to her like bees to honey.

She was first of all a wife and mother. She and Daddy adored each other and daily demonstrated their affection in many little ways. Even with eight children, there was more than enough love to go around. Mother had a delightful way of making each of us feel very special. As we grew older we were encouraged to develop our gifts with never a suggestion we were limited in any way. Everything was possible, but it had to be earned.

Running a household of ten took most of her time and energy. Because of her full schedule at home, Mother had only two regular activities that directly involved Koreans. One was a Sunday school class for women in one of the town's five churches, and the other was running the Self-help Work Department of the Po Sung Girls' School. She loved to embroider and taught it to those who needed money for room, board, and tuition.

Every fifth day was market day when people from the country brought their produce and goods to town. As often as possible she went to explore its possibilities. Always on the lookout for dress or shirt material, she carried a tape measure in her purse. One day she discovered a bull cart displaying a dead tiger right in the middle of the market. The mountains in North Korea are known for some of the largest tigers in the world. This one looked huge, so she got out her tape to measure its paw. From the end of the longest toe to the pug it measured eighteen inches, indeed a very big beast. For the Korean practicing folk medicine, the parts most valued were the claws, whiskers, and liver—really strong stuff!

Knowing the challenges, Mother was extremely interested in the Korean women, whose lives were much harder than her own. She frequently stopped to talk with them, particularly those with babies and little children. Conversing with one, Mother asked about her family. An infant slept on her back and several tots clung to her skirts, peering up at the strange person with odd white skin and blue eyes.

"I have two children," the woman said. "How many do you have?"

"I have been blessed with four," Mother responded, "but if you have only two, are these others your neighbors' children?"

"No," she said, "I gave birth to them, but they haven't had the smallpox."

Vaccine had not yet come to Korea, and the disease was such a scourge that families didn't count their children until they had survived it. Many faces were deeply scarred. "You'll have a pock mark on your face for every grain of rice left in your bowl!" was the parental threat to a child slow in finishing his food. As soon as the vaccine became available the disease virtually disappeared.

As time passed Mother saw more and more practical ways to help the women. The year Molly went off to boarding school she embarked on a special brand of missionary work she'd been aching to do for years.

Daddy had a regular schedule for visiting churches outside of Syenchun. One of the largest cities was Sin Weiju, fifty miles north on the Yalu River; and Mother accompanied him when he went there. After several days he proceeded on to other towns and villages while Mother stayed behind with friend Paik-si Wirun.

In the morning they held Bible study classes that were packed every day. Christianity was joyfully accepted. Its doctrines granted new, elevated status to women who had long been mere chattels with little freedom or dignity. Afternoons were given over to household helps and evenings dedicated to prenatal classes.

Mother bravely tackled an important sanitation problem. Korean winter clothing was heavily padded and had to be taken completely apart for cleaning. The old cotton stuffing was discarded, the cloth washed, and the garment reassembled with new filling.

The average person was fortunate to have more than one set per season, and because of its construction, nothing was washed all winter. There was no such thing as dry cleaning. Since they didn't use underwear, just imagine how their clothing reeked before spring arrived. Strangely enough, nearly every household had a Singer sewing machine, so Mother, the practical soul, had hundreds of patterns made and distributed for BVDs in large, medium, and small sizes for men, bloomers for women and girls, and underpants for boys. She urged the women to make several undergarments of light-weight cotton for each member of the family. They could be washed and dried in the home during the winter, and presto, benefits for all.

A young Korean girl was pampered and petted until the age of five when she was pressed into taking care of younger siblings, helping with household chores, and learning her place as a female. From then on her life was difficult. As soon as she reached puberty a marriage was arranged, and she became the slave of her mother-in-law, a kindhearted one being the exception. She had a hard life, but when her son was old enough to take a wife, she could rest and work her daughter-in-law as she had been worked. It was an accepted cycle.

Every now and then a young matron managed a bit of free time for herself, so Mother made up recipes for treats that could be concocted from locally available ingredients. She had a large-sized sweet tooth and felt sure they did too. She also had made and passed out dozens of checkers games which were quickly copied. She taught them to play, and the pastime became a huge success.

Most gratifying to her was teaching prenatal classes. Mother had no medical training, but with her record of eight living babies and no losses, she was definitely a person of authority. When she announced the course, many were eager to attend. Knowing that the Korean mother-in-law was boss, she invited women whose daughters-in-law were expecting babies. The future mothers could come if they wished, but because they had no real control over their lives, Mother wanted to give her message to those in charge.

First she stressed a good diet. No longer was the young woman to eat leftovers from the family table. She must have a balanced diet of rice, vegetables, fruit, and a little meat. She shouldn't lift or carry anything heavy. Most homes had no running water. It was drawn from a well with a bucket and rope, poured into an earthenware jug, and carried home, usually balanced on the daughter-in-law's head. Somebody else should do that task while she was pregnant. And finally, she should wear loose-fitting clothes that were good for both mother and baby. Such ideas were revolutionary, but when given by a woman who had done so well, they were surely worth trying.

"If I advised standing on their heads for fifteen minutes a day, they would probably have done that too," Mother joked.

When she returned the following year, many women came to class bringing beautiful, healthy babies.

"*Nam Pueen-nim* (honorable Mrs. Lampe)," they told her, "we did just as you said. A thousand thanks."

Pyeng Yang Foreign School

But continue . . . in the things which you have learned and been assured of, knowing of whom you have learned them.
II Tim. 3:14

The boarding school where all of us went at the age of twelve was founded by the Presbyterian and Methodist missions for the education of their children. Those from the business and diplomatic communities were welcome, but they were few in number. The sprawling campus was located in one of the Presbyterian compounds.

A two-and-a-half story red brick building accommodated all classrooms, the library, the science lab, and the principal's office. Across the street were a multipurpose gym and playing field. Up the hill were the principal's residence, boys' and girls' dorms with two clay tennis courts in front of them, and the infirmary. The walk to class was about the length of a city block. Homes and gardens bordered the pretty campus set with lots of trees. The whole compound was surrounded by a wall, enclosing a little bit of America.

The student body of about 150 attended from kindergarten through high school. In later years 50 percent were from China, and 20 percent were day students who lived at home. PYFS was not accredited by the U.S. Association of Colleges and Universities because it didn't have a large enough library or properly equipped science lab, but that didn't keep graduates from going to colleges of their choice. Along with an application, the principal sent a letter of recommendation, suggesting they check the performance of previous graduates who had done well in major colleges and universities. No student was ever turned down. PYFS had the finest reputation of any school in Asia.

Upperclassmen had very little room for electives. It was a straight college prep course to make sure everyone would be academically equipped no matter where he went. Additionally, there were requirements for physical education and Bible study and options such as chorus and band.

Mornings began with a thirty-minute chapel. Usually the principal spoke, but once a week one of the faculty gave a talk. I was deeply impressed when Mr. Murphy told of his thrilling experience in evangelism.

"Every day," he said, "I go down to the main road and preach. Many men and women pass that way, and one by one I engage them in conversation and present the Gospel. If one rejects the Good News, I try another and keep trying until I have at least one convert." Could anything be more wonderful than that? I thought about Daddy. He was a preacher, but he never talked about such things. On our next vacation I told him about Mr. Murphy's evangelistic ministry and how he wouldn't quit for the day until he had converted at least one person to Christ.

"How many people have you converted?" I asked.

"Oh, I've never converted anyone," he answered. I was crushed! My father must be a complete failure. "Fran, conversion is the work of the Holy Spirit. I preach the Word; the Holy Spirit does the rest. I would not presume to take the credit." What a man! How fortunate I was to call this wonderful, humble person Father.

Back at school not many weeks later, the Reverend Mr. Bill Shaw, a Methodist missionary, preached a powerful sermon: "You can't really start to live until you settle your eternal future with God." At the end of the service I prayed the "sinner's prayer" and began my journey as a child of the King. No whistles or bells, nor were there floods of joy. I simply knew I had taken the step that sealed my future once and for all, and I was glad. Looking back across the sixty years since, I see how He has protected, guided, chastised, and loved me. Some of the worst times have been seasons of growing. I didn't like them, but I learned from them. In moving all over the Far East and the United States I discovered that His family is everywhere. There was always a Christian community to welcome me, no exceptions.

Classes started at 8:00 a.m. and ended at 3:00 p.m. with an hour for lunch. Dorm students had two forty-five-minute classroom study periods after supper. Yes, sir, we were there to learn, and it was serious business; but we had a lot of fun too.

Two or three times during the winter we could go skating when the moon was full and the rink was frozen solid. Study hall was held in the afternoon, and we partied at night. My, it was romantic! A Victrola provided the music, and a big bonfire kept us from freezing. We drank endless cups of hot cocoa poured from a huge pot and ate apples skewered on chopsticks and dipped in melted *yut* (taffy). Not very good for my braces. How Dr. McAnlis scolded. I had wobbly ankles, but crossing arms with one of the boys and skating to the Blue Danube Waltz made me feel like a champion. Life just couldn't get much better.

It's painful to remember how my years at boarding school started. We rode to the station in the car, packed all around with suitcases, boxes, and bags. It was exciting to be old enough to join the big kids at school, and I was all set with new bedding, clothes, and everything I needed to get started.

Mother couldn't come to get me settled in, but Hunkey promised to help, and she was sister/mother to all of us younger ones. I was okay until we neared the station and I realized I wasn't going home again. Jimmy and Molly got their platform tickets punched and carried the lighter bundles, but all I wanted was to stay close to Mother.

Daddy checked the trunks and coreys (telescoping baskets) into the baggage car, and the rest of us climbed into the third-class car. Amid the hustle and confusion I began to feel a big lump in my throat, and when Hunkey yelled at me to hurry to get seats that were together, lead weights held my feet.

Some of the boxes went into the overhead racks; smaller ones we tucked under the seats. The train master's whistle sounded. Jimmy and Molly turned toward the door as Mother gave each of us a kiss. When she hugged me, I could hold it in no longer. I flung my arms around her neck and broke into heaving sobs. Another blast on the whistle.

"I don't want to go!" I screamed as Mother pulled my arms away. "Please let me stay home!"

"Sweet, precious girl," she comforted as she kissed my tear-streaked face, "try it for a few weeks, then if you still want to come home, you may," I nodded my agreement, but shook with quiet sobs as the train pulled out and the family disappeared.

She was right. The new world of boarding school was different but not difficult. I felt well prepared in classwork, and keeping to dorm schedules was second nature because of the discipline at home. It was exciting to be with so many my own age. I liked it as my wise mother had known I would.

My years there were wonderful, and there were *boys*, one or two of whom were special each year. Knowing human nature and the cunning of youth, the teachers kept a close eye on us. Even holding hands was looked on as being "fast," and kissing was simply out of the question. We didn't.

In the boarders' dining room they posted a new seating chart every two weeks. We sat at long tables accommodating twelve with a teacher at the head. The constant rotation helped us get to know all the other students and kept cliques from forming. It was a red-letter day when the matron arranged for us to sit with special friends.

The food was never as good as what we enjoyed at home, but it was wholesome and predictable. On certain days there were specials. Wednesday morning we had cereal made from a variety of beans boiled together into a glutinous mass we called ladybugs and beetles. Sounds dreadful, but I liked it, and we had brown sugar with it—a real treat.

Thursday night we had Chinese or Korean food, rotating three or four dishes, one of which was *man-du-gook.* Its base was a soup in which vegetable-filled dumplings had been simmered along with water chestnuts and bits of meat. The boys called the dumplings skinned rats, trying to spoil our appetite, hoping they could have our share. It never bothered me.

Friday night was birthday night, which meant a big cake and ice cream arrived at every table. We sang the birthday song for each student celebrating that week—the same tune several times over until Sarah Newland composed a new one that we alternated with the old. Here it is.

Adam Had A Birthday

Dorm life was filled with rules and routines that we protested, but then it was the thing to do.

We were required to keep our rooms clean with beds made and everything put away before class. It was hard for some of the younger ones to remember at first, but there was a remedy. After the blessing was offered at lunch, the names of all offenders were called. They had to leave and tidy up their rooms before they could eat. Once or twice, and it didn't happen again.

Saturdays were free after we passed room inspection. In preparation we changed beds, listed the laundry and put it in bags outside the door, arranged drawers and closets neatly, dusted everything and swept the floor. It was a genuine white-glove inspection, so again the new students often had to try more than once to make the grade. At the end of the year everybody who had an average mark of ninety or better had a dinner consisting of a huge serving of strawberry shortcake. Anticipation of the treat was enough to keep us trying all year long.

The only time brothers and sisters got together was when we walked the mile and a half to the seminary to worship on Sunday afternoon. Korean churches met in the morning, so the English language service was held in the afternoon, allowing missionaries to attend. We could also sit together for supper that night.

Early in my freshman year we got the first of three typhoid shots. It was one of the miseries we had to endure every third year. The next day I began having a reaction during church. My head ached, my heart was pounding, and I felt I was burning up. I put my head on Betty's shoulder, and she put her arm around me. If I'd been younger nobody could have taken Mother's place, but Betty was there and knew just what I needed. After the service Betty and Jim walked me straight to the infirmary. The nurse took my temperature and found it was 104. The matron immediately checked me in, and I was glad just to shut my eyes and sleep it off.

My worst stay at the infirmary was for the mumps. Since it was going through school like wildfire, I wasn't surprised to feel a lump behind my right ear one morning.

"I have read that the severity and duration of the disease can be reduced by X-raying the area. If you're willing I'd like you to go to the hospital to get a dose on each side," the school doctor said.

I wasn't feeling in the least ill, and wanting to get this business over with as quickly as possible, I agreed. The treatment not only didn't work, it made things worse. I never remember being so sick. I swelled all over. My ears were in pockets, and the swelling extended all the way to my waist and down to my elbows. I couldn't get my mouth open, and my temperature never went below 104 for four days. The principal telegraphed Mother to come if she could, and I was thankful to have her nurse me through the worst of it.

A few of the teachers were from the local missionary community, but most of the faculty came from the States on two-year contracts, which they often extended for a second, third, or fourth time. Friends, advisors, and caregivers, they were much more than teachers. If we were homesick, they comforted. If we were unruly, they brought the offenders to book in no uncertain terms. The rules seemed strict, but they were fair and applied to all.

A favorite teacher was Mr. Sam Wong, a Korean who had graduated from and was a professor at Oregon State University before he came to teach lab sciences and PE. One of the boys in Hunkey's class loved chemistry, so Mr. Wong gave him extra assignments and challenging work beyond the regular curriculum. When he got to college he was tested and advanced a year. A huge bonus.

Students in the upper grades were permitted to go off campus without chaperones on weekends. Boys could go alone, girls in groups of two or more. Any junior or senior having at least a B average studied in the dorm rather than the supervised study hall. A little at a time we were given greater privileges and responsibilities that made the transition to college in the States the natural next step.

The class of 1940 began with four of us in the eighth grade.

Mary Chapman, a redhead, came from Japan. Claire Torrey, with coal-black hair and blue eyes, arrived from China as did brown-haired David Owens, our one and only boy. I was a platinum blonde from Korea.

The student body and faculty, Sept. 1939

Each year more joined, and we ended our senior year with twenty-three, the largest class and the last ever to graduate from PYFS. Two classmates were White Russians from Harbin, Manchuria. Jack Liberman was outgoing; Joe Weiner was his shadow and very quiet. It wasn't until we had a reunion forty-four years later in Montreat, North Carolina, that I learned the circumstances of Joe's coming.

His father was a successful banker in Harbin, a gathering place for many stateless Russian Jews. Wanting the best possible education for his son, he had investigated all boarding schools in the Far East. Six months before Joe was to start at PYFS, Mr. Weiner died. Nevertheless, Joe's mother sent him off to school. He had travel documents permitting him to leave Manchuria and enter Korea, and there should have been no problem as both countries were under Japanese occupation. All went well until he reached the border. There a Japanese official claimed the papers were not in order and made Joe leave the train.

"It will take a day or two to straighten this out," he said, taking him into his office. "You can stay here in the station," he went on, pointing to a room with hard benches," or you may come to my house." Noticing Joe's tennis racket he added, "There is a school with some tennis courts next door. You can play if you wish."

" I'd like stay at your house. Thank you," Joe said.

The next day he found some Chinese students with whom to play tennis and had a good time but grew concerned when by that evening there was still no clearance. This continued for several days. In the meantime, Joe's mother learned he had not shown up in Pyeng Yang and was frantic. Several Russian children had disappeared recently without a trace while riding Manchurian trains. She was sick with worry and tried desperately to find out what had happened to him. Nothing. Relatives traveled back and forth on the trains going to Korea searching for any clue to his whereabouts. Nothing!

At the end of the fourth day the Japanese official had a proposal for Joe. "As you can see, I have no wife, but with all my heart I want a son. Your father is dead. I would like to adopt you and take you to Japan when I return in a few months. Will you consider it?"

"It is very kind of you," Joe answered, "but I want to finish my education. I will think about your offer, and when I come back through in December I will let you know."

Disappointed but willing to accept Joe's decision, he handed him his papers, which had indeed been cleared, and put him on the next train. By the time Joe crossed the border again at Christmas the official was gone.

Along with good times came sad ones. A new student, Bob Irwin, from Cheefoo, China, didn't like boarding school. He was a quiet little fellow with slicked-down dark hair, sad eyes, and ears that stood out like sails. Nobody knew how much he missed his family or how desperately he wanted to go home.

Railroad tracks ran along the bottom of a long, low hill behind the school. One night Bob slipped out, went over the hill, and climbed the fence next to them. At five miles from the main station, the express headed for China was up to speed when it reached the point where Bob stood. He jumped to grab the handrails at the door of a car and missed. The handrails hit him on the side of the head, killing him instantly, tossing his body away from the train.

The next day we gasped with shock and horror when his death was announced at chapel. How was it that we hadn't sensed his grief and pain?

Mary Chapman and I volunteered to make a wreath as a gift from our class because there was no place to buy one. We bought yellow and white mums and greenery, some chicken wire, and ribbon. Several of us worked on it, and the result was beautiful. Bob's father came for the funeral then took the body home for burial.

That was our only accidental death, but we lost another through illness. Betsy Larsen began to suffer severe headaches. During Christmas vacation the mission doctor in her home station discovered a brain tumor. She had surgery but didn't survive the operation. We lost still another for political reasons. Inge was a beautiful tall blonde. Her father, a diplomat posted in Harbin, was ordered back to Lithuania at the time of its annexation by Russia. There was no choice; she had to go too. Stories and rumors abounded about what went on when that country was taken over. Inge was such a lovely, outgoing person. We hated to think that anything bad would happen to her. We never heard.

Our graduating class, 1940

In the fall of our senior year they decided to let our class take a week's trip to someplace special. We chose the Diamond Mountains, a spectacularly beautiful, rugged range that crosses the Korean peninsula. The only ways to go through them were by foot or sedan chair. The main pathway runs from one end to the other, with dozens of side trails to picturesque temples, peaks, and waterfalls.

We took the train to the western end of the range, left our baggage at a little inn, and set off on a quick trip along one of the trails. In the valley we saw a huge carving of Buddha on a rock face of black granite. Every turn in the path seemed more spectacular than the one before. The dark weathered rock surfaces were a perfect background to the splashes of crimson, orange, and yellow of mid-October's turning leaves. It seemed as if God had worked overtime to create such beauty.

As you might expect, boys and girls paired off to enjoy the occasion. My particular interest of the moment was Billy Linton. We were the last couple to head back to the inn. Just ahead of us were a teacher and a classmate, Tinsley Bradley. The path overhung the steeply sloping rock face, about thirty feet above a dry river bed full of huge boulders. The guardrail had been bent down parallel to the path and gave no protection. There was no danger going single file, but with Miss Souers on the outside, she and Tinsley were walking side by side when she slipped. At her cry of alarm Billy and I looked up just in time to see her go head first off the path. In trying to grab her, Tinsley lost his balance and went flying after her. They hit the sloping surface and rolled about five yards before becoming wedged under an enormous boulder.

Within two minutes we found a way to climb down to them. Tinsley had landed on his shoulder and was on top. He was just a little dazed, and we pulled him off. Miss Souers, wearing glasses, had instinctively raised her arm to protect her eyes and landed squarely on her elbow. Helping her was a different matter. We edged her out from under the rock and saw that her arm was twisted in a strange way. I gently tried to turn it, but there was a bone protruding at her elbow. She would need extra help getting back to the inn.

"Billy, you stay here, and I'll go," I said.

"Okay," he agreed, and I was off and running down the path a mile and a half to the village. They found a stretcher, and all the boys volunteered to come along. In short order Miss Souers was rescued, but that ended the fun for her. She and one of the other teachers were on the next train for Pyeng Yang. Billy and I felt we had done heroic work that day.

All through the trip we stayed in Japanese inns, where large rooms were available for groups such as ours. Characteristically, a narrow passageway ran along the side of the room, and there we left our shoes. We slept on a raised platform covered by finely woven bamboo mat with padding underneath. Accommodating so many was not easy, but we made the best of it. If there were two rooms, we divided up by gender; but on Pirribong, the highest mountain, there was just one long room for all of us. No problem. The girls occupied one end and the boys the other with the teachers in the middle. It was a tight squeeze that night and not comfortable because it was so cold.

The inn was located about a thousand feet below the summit. We were told we shouldn't miss the sunrise, so those of us who were morning people crept out from under the blankets and reached the top at first light. We were surprised to see at least two hundred already there, waiting quietly. As the first thin sliver of sun appeared, the mountaintop erupted with the sound of Buddhist monks and nuns chanting the rosary.

The vista changed moment by moment as new light reached out and brought to life one peak after another. The spectacular sight held us spellbound. Then shivering with the cold, we hurried back to get our hands around a cup of hot tea.

Indescribable beauty was everywhere, and a new sense of freedom lifted my spirits. I was strong and experienced only a comfortable weariness after climbing all day. I felt a hunger for good food and a yearning to learn more of what was really important. It was a good time, one of the best in my life.

At the end of the week we were back in our dorms, and like all students, dreading exams and term papers, counting the days until Christmas vacation.

Almost before we knew it, June arrived. Each of us was headed for college, setting out to conquer the world.[1] Graduation from PYFS was a bit different. We didn't have caps and gowns, but the girls wore long white dresses and the boys dark suits and ties. The women in the community made each girl a beautiful bouquet of roses freshly cut from their gardens. As we took that last long walk down the aisle and up the steps to the dais, I had a lump in my throat almost too big to bear. These were my friends. For years we had shared life's best and worst moments, and soon they would all be gone. Joy and sadness, anticipation and wonder—it was all there. It was there, and then it was gone. Tomorrow? It just had to be even better!

---

[1] From our class came three medical doctors; four foreign missionaries; three ministers; one colonel in the army; one lawyer. Three married professors; two married businessmen; one married a doctor; and Jack and Joe became successful entrepreneurs.

The Emperor's Gift

Desire realized is sweet to the soul.
Prov. 13:19

"Well, girls," Daddy said, " enjoy yourselves. It will probably be the only time in your lives when you'll have a week's trip and a buying spree that won't cost a cent."

"And do be careful," Mother added as she hugged us.

"We will; please don't worry." We hurried to climb aboard the train.

It was a new experience. Betty had been in the States for two years, but this was the first time I'd left the country, totally away from the protection of my parents. It was exciting, but the best part was that in ten days we'd be back to the safety of home and family. How could I face leaving for America next month?

Our adventure began one midnight in late June 1940 when we pulled out of Syenchun station for the twenty-four hour journey to Peking. Because we were traveling alone, Daddy treated us to second-class coach seats, an extravagance at five dollars each but well worth the price for the cleaner, less crowded car. The arms and headrests of the blue plush seats were protected with embroidered, starched, white cotton covers. It wasn't quite as grand as first class, decorated in red with matching curtains, but a huge improvement over third class with its crush of people, dirty green seats, crying babies, and trash on the floor.

We felt elegant as we stowed our suitcases in the overhead racks and made ourselves comfortable for the night. Betty had returned to spend the summer after her third year of college. In the fall she'd accompany me to the States where I too would attend college.

I'm a freshman at Knox College. My picture for the Rogues' Gallery.

"Did you ever in your life see such a wide-open plain?" Betty remarked as we ate breakfast in the dining car the next morning. "Look, it's just a solid carpet of rice fields from here to the horizon!" All day the train sped on with nothing to relieve the flatness but a few mounded graves in family cemeteries and an occasional cluster of houses and trees.

Manchuria was one giant rice bowl. Declared by the Japanese to be a colony in 1931, they forced Korean farmers to relocate there to grow food for them, claiming they needed it to feed their people. In the summer of 1937, they went to war with China, taking and holding the major coastal cities and the capital, Nanking. But their economic problems began to worsen. They had grabbed the Chinese tiger by the tail and couldn't let go.

The Japanese declared all currency in occupied China and Korea to be of equal value to the yen, yet we could get four times more for the U.S. dollar in occupied China than in Korea. Opportunities for making money at their expense were numerous, and in effect, they were paying for our trip. Oh sweet retribution!

As soon as the banks opened on our first day in Peking, Betty and I each cashed a fifty-dollar U.S. check and received currency at the rate of sixteen Chinese dollars to one U.S. Through the bank (and quite legally) we both sent Daddy, at par, the Korean equivalent of fifty dollars, paid for a week's lodging and food at a missionary guest house, and had mountains of money left. The paper money was huge, almost twice the size of U.S. currency, and each denomination was printed in a different color. Best of all were the red ones with elaborately engraved dragons running all around the edges.

The week following was pure, unadulterated joy. Each morning we hired rickshaws to take us sightseeing, shopping, and to every variety of restaurant. Peking was full of contrasts. The wide, high walls of the inner city with their enormous gates looked quite forbidding. Masses of people in a perpetual hurry pushed and shoved their way along. Hawkers sold all kinds of wares, clanging old shears or beating out a rhythm with sticks to attract attention. The air reeked of roasting sweet potatoes, frying garlic, and the ever-present "honey carts" with their loads of human waste.

And there were children, always the children with their dark eyes and curious glances. They ran about mostly naked on those warm June days. Many of the smaller girls wore their hair in topknots tied up with bright bits of yarn. Some had theirs braided on either side and joined in a loop at the crown. One evening at dinner our host told us why mothers concocted such hairdos for the little ones. If a child should fall and be in danger of her life, they believed an angel would reach down and snatch her up to heaven by the hair before she could slide down into hell. The braid "handle" made doubly sure the angel wouldn't miss.

We never tired of visiting the beautiful temples and palaces with gold, blue, or green-tiled roofs, cool, spacious halls, and shaded grounds. The European influence had brought in fine hotels where elegant ladies and handsome men attended tea dances and swank evening parties. With all that money, shopping was heady business. Guided by my sister, I bought things suitable for my first year in college and gifts for the family. Mother had asked us to get some things for Willard, now serving in his first church. Though living on a limited income, he wanted a present for his bride. In his letter he wrote, "I'm enclosing a sketch of a fur coat for Charlotte. If there is any money left over, please pick out a set of cloisonné (a low, shallow flower bowl and four candle holders), and if by great good fortune there is anything more left, we'd like to have a few sets to give to friends." Enclosed was a check for fifty dollars.

We chose a reputable furrier and selected matched baby-leopard skins for a beautiful coat with a full swagger back, rolled collar, and wide sleeves, exactly like the drawing. Three days later when it was ready, we cashed Willard's check and were delighted to find the exchange rate had gone up to twenty to one. After we paid the bill, there was enough left over to buy not one, but five additional cloisonné sets.

On our last day in Peking, with our own last copper spent, we went to the bank to send the balance of Willard's money to Daddy in Syenchun. We changed the Chinese equivalent of U.S. $18.65 into Korean currency and sent it to Korea, where it magically expanded to U.S. $75.42, a splendid gift of His Imperial Majesty,

Hirohito, emperor of Japan!

By the end of 1931 the army was in control of Japan's political life. The Kwantung Army had completed its conquest of Manchuria. Henry Pu-yi, the last of the Imperial Manchu dynasty, had been spirited away from his home in Tientsin by Colonel Itagaki and virtually at gun point had been told he was to be the head of a new country called Manchukuo, Chinese for Manchu Country. In February 1932, with Kwantung Army advisors on all sides, Henry Pu-yi solemnly declared the "independence" of Manchukuo from China. Japan now had a new colony (Edwin P. Hoyt, *Japan's Wars, 1853-1952,* New York: McGraw-Hill, 1986, 97).

An End and a Beginning

For I know the plans I have for you, declares the Lord,
plans for welfare and not for calamity
to give you a future and a hope.
Jer. 29:11

The summer of 1940 ended too soon and not soon enough. It was a time of mixed emotions—sadness at leaving the family and all that I knew and loved and eager anticipation of what lay ahead. My five older brothers and sisters had written of the wonders of life in the United States. I could hardly wait to experience them for myself.

For a time I considered going to Yenjing University in Peking, where enough courses were offered in English for me to take a full load. I'd be just twenty-four hours away by train so I could go home for Christmas, and I'd have the unique cultural experience of living in a dorm with Chinese students. The lure of going to America won out, and I soon gave up the idea.

We left Sorai Beach early that year. As soon as I finished packing everything I was taking to college, I climbed Tai Mok San, the highest peak on the west edge of Syenchun, and looked at everything carefully. I wanted to remember it all. Each of us had one summer trip home during college, so I wasn't really saying a final good-bye. That made me feel a little better. On my last day at home Daddy and I were in the side yard looking at his cherry tree. The fruit had been carefully picked, pitted, and canned for Daddy's favorite dessert.

"Frances, I have something I want to say to you before you leave," he said. I knew it was serious because he usually called me Fran. "I know you'll do whatever you think right when you get to the States and make your own decisions, but I believe you'll be a much happier person if you neither smoke nor drink," he continued.

Three of the family already there smoked, but I didn't know about the drinking. For me, the choice was easy. I had a deep love and respect for my parents and couldn't bear to disappoint them in any way. I was certain they knew what was best for me and trusted their judgment. No promises were made, but in my own mind it was settled. I wouldn't smoke or drink, period. And I never have. I haven't regretted the decision. At the time there were no warnings about smoking, but it was expensive, and on my thirty-five-dollar-a-month mission allowance for everything beyond board, room, and tuition, it was going to be a squeeze. As for drinking, I never could figure out why people did. It tastes terrible. With many nonalcoholic choices, the decision was not difficult.

After a week of travel to Japan and doing some sightseeing, Betty and I arrived at dockside in Yokohama to board the *Heian Maru.* It was a cargo ship that also accommodated about 120 passengers. We were booked to share a cabin with Margie Lutz, another college mish kid spending the summer with her family in Korea.

I looked up at the ship that would take us to the States and felt stuck half way between the past and the future. Why did I feel hesitant about leaving? (Mother told me I was reluctant to come into this world—of her eight babies, I was the only forceps delivery.) I had fought going to Pyeng Yang, and now college was the big unknown.

We moved slowly in the passport inspection line. Donkey engines groaned as huge cranes lifted netloads of cargo from the dock, up over the deck, and down into the hold. Trucks backed up to cargo doors to deliver food. Every new step I'd taken was good, beyond anything I'd dreamed possible, and I was conscious that God had directed every one. Surely this was no exception.

During that last talk with Daddy under the cherry tree he said, "Fran, there will be times when things won't go smoothly, and we won't be there to guide you. But you're strong, and never ever forget God's promises you've learned from the Bible: 'I will be with you; I will not fail you nor forsake you,' and 'Be strong and courageous! Do not tremble or be dismayed, for the Lord your God is with you wherever you go.'"

At last we were cleared to board. I had a strong sense of the moment's importance. I really was beginning a new season of my life. When the ship pulled away from the dock, nothing would ever be the same. Would I be disappointed or find things better than I ever imagined?" Being an optimist, I was sure it would be the latter.

Shrugging off fear, I gripped the railing with one hand, my purse with the other, and climbed the wobbly gangplank. As I neared the top I looked up into the eyes of the handsomest man I'd ever seen. He was slender, of medium height with light brown wavy hair, and the most beautiful dark eyes. He smiled and reached for my hand to help me over the top step. My heart did a flip-flop, and *yes*, life was going to be good indeed!

Mother and Daddy, 1950

That man was Kedar Bryan, son of an American lawyer in Shanghai. He too was on his way to the States to attend the University of North Carolina in Chapel Hill, a thousand miles away from Galesburg. We were friends immediately but tried to be sensible about getting serious. The heart, however, has a way of overruling the head. In 1942, with World War II raging and his parents interned by the Japanese, we borrowed a little money and were married.

The End

Two Bamboos, the story of our life together is in progress. It tells of our adventures all over the Far East, including three evacuations and forty-two moves.

The title comes from the term "Bamboo Americans" as U.S. citizens born and reared in the Far East are sometimes called.

Final Note

Joseph Lamp, my grandfather, was born in 1837 in the village of Rojendorf on the Kiel Canal in Schleswig-Holstein. At the age of fifteen he emigrated to the United States to avoid Bismarck's draft into the German army. His first employment was in a logging camp in Michigan, where he received a grand salary of seventy-two dollars a year plus board and keep.

On his trips to the forests Conrad Baker got to know Joseph and hired him to work in his lumber yard in Wataga, Illinois. One evening they went to a revival meeting, where both accepted Christ.

Conrad urged Joseph to get an education, but before entering Knox College, he had to finish high school. He went on to Union Theological Seminary in New York City, a Presbyterian institution at that time. He did it all while working to support himself. He had to study late into the night, and to avoid falling asleep, he built a high desk at which he had to stand.

Upon graduation he pastored Christ Presbyterian Church on 34th Street at Tenth Avenue. Now a warehouse, it was a mission church supported by the wealthy, uptown Brick Presbyterian Church. Soon after taking up his duties there, he returned to Galesburg to marry Emma Willard on September 20, 1877. In a double wedding, Emma's sister, Lila, married Thomas Winn.

Joseph earned a Ph.D. from New York University and in 1896 went to Omaha Theological Seminary to teach Hebrew and lecture in theology. There he founded the Dundee Presbyterian Church. His wife and their three sons were charter members.

Somewhere along the line he changed his name. Joseph Lamp (the German spelling) became Joseph Joachim Lampe. He must have thought the additions lent an air of distinction befitting his achievements. Henry, my father was the eldest of their seven children. One daughter, Cordelia, died at the age of ten. When Henry was a teenager, all six children came down with diphtheria, and within two weeks three of them died. Daddy, Willard, and William lived through it.

The three surviving brothers became Presbyterian ministers, but each was called to a different ministry. Daddy served as a missionary for forty years. Willard founded the School of Religion at the University of Iowa, Iowa City. Bill pastored several churches, serving for thirty-six years at West Presbyterian Church in St. Louis, Missouri. He was moderator of the the Presbyterian Church, (U.S.A) for a year during World War II.

Uncle Willard, Uncle Bill,Grandmother, Grandfather,and Daddy